Jesus, the Apostles,
and the Early Church

POPE BENEDICT XVI

Jesus, the Apostles, and the Early Church

General Audiences
15 March 2006—14 February 2007

IGNATIUS PRESS   SAN FRANCISCO

English translations by *L'Osservatore Romano*

Cover art:
Christ appearing to the Apostles on the Lake of Tiberias
(From the upper section of the *Maesta* altarpiece)
Duccio di Buoninsegna (c. 1260–1319)
Museo dell'Opera Metropolitana, Siena, Italy
© Scala / Art Resource, New York

Papal coat of arms image by www.AgnusImages.com

Cover design by Roxanne Mei Lum

© 2007 by Libreria Editrice Vaticana, Vatican City

CONTENTS

1   Christ and the Church / *15 March 2006*   7

2   "Witnesses of Christ" / *22 March 2006*   12

3   The Gift of "Communion" / *29 March 2006*   16

4   "Safeguarding the Gift" / *5 April 2006*   20

5   Communion in Time: Tradition / *26 April 2006*   24

6   The Apostolic Tradition of
the Church / *3 May 2006*   29

7   Having a "Vision from on High" / *10 May 2006*   34

8   Peter, the Fisherman / *17 May 2006*   39

9   Peter, the Apostle / *24 May 2006*   44

10   Peter, the Rock / *7 June 2006*   50

11   Andrew, the Protoclete / *14 June 2006*   54

12   James, the Greater / *21 June 2006*   60

13   James, the Lesser / *28 June 2006*   63

14   John, Son of Zebedee / *5 July 2006*   67

15   John, the Theologian / *9 August 2006*   71

16   John, the Seer of Patmos / *23 August 2006*   76

17   Matthew / *30 August 2006*   81

18 Philip, the Apostle / *6 September 2006*   86

19 Thomas the Twin / *27 September 2006*   91

20 Bartholomew / *4 October 2006*   96

21 Simon and Jude / *11 October 2006*   100

22 Judas Iscariot and Matthias / *18 October 2006*   104

23 Paul of Tarsus / *25 October 2006*   109

24 Saint Paul's New Outlook / *8 November 2006*   114

25 Saint Paul and the Spirit / *15 November 2006*   119

26 Saint Paul and the Church / *22 November 2006*   124

27 Timothy and Titus / *13 December 2006*   128

28 Stephen, the Protomartyr / *10 January 2007*   134

29 Barnabas, Silas (Also Called Silvanus), and
    Apollos / *31 January 2007*   139

30 Priscilla and Aquila / *7 February 2007*   145

31 Women at the Service of the
    Gospel / *14 February 2007*   150

SCRIPTURE INDEX   155

Christ and the Church

Dear Brothers and Sisters,

Following the Catecheses on the Psalms and Canticles of Lauds and of Vespers, I would like to dedicate the upcoming Wednesday Audiences to the mystery of the relationship between Christ and the Church, reflecting upon it from the experience of the Apostles, in light of the duty entrusted to them.

The Church was built on the foundation of the Apostles as a community of faith, hope, and charity. Through the Apostles, we come to Jesus himself. The Church begins to establish herself when some fishermen of Galilee meet Jesus, allowing themselves to be won over by his gaze, his voice, his warm and strong invitation: "Follow me, and I will make you become fishers of men" (Mk 1:17; Mt 4:19).

At the start of the third millennium, my beloved Predecessor John Paul II invited the Church to contemplate the Face of Christ (cf. *Novo Millennio Ineunte*, nos. 16ff.). Continuing in the same direction, I would like to show, in the Catechesis that I begin today, how it is precisely the light of that Face that is reflected on the face of the Church (cf. *Lumen Gentium*, no. 1), notwithstanding the limits and shadows of our fragile and sinful humanity.

After Mary, a pure reflection of the light of Christ, it is from the Apostles, through their word and witness, that we receive the truth of Christ. Their mission is not isolated, however, but is situated within a mystery of communion that involves the entire People of God and is carried out in stages from the Old to the New Covenant.

In this regard, it must be said that the message of Jesus is completely misunderstood if it is separated from the context of the faith and hope of the Chosen People: like John the Baptist, his direct Precursor, Jesus above all addresses Israel (cf. Mt 15:24) in order to "gather" it together in the eschatological time that arrived with him. And like that of John, the preaching of Jesus is at the same time a call of grace and a sign of contradiction and of justice for the entire People of God.

And so, from the first moment of his salvific activity, Jesus of Nazareth strives to gather together the People of God. Even if his preaching is always an appeal for personal conversion, in reality he continually aims to build the People of God whom he came to bring together, purify, and save.

As a result, therefore, an individualistic interpretation of Christ's proclamation of the Kingdom, specific to liberal theology, is unilateral and without foundation, as a great liberal theologian, Adolf von Harnack, summed it up in the year 1900 in his lessons on *The essence of Christianity*: "The Kingdom of God, insofar as it comes in *single* individuals, is able to enter their soul and is welcomed by them. The Kingdom of God is the *dominion* of God, certainly, but it is the dominion of the holy God in individual hearts" (cf. Third Lesson, 100ff.).

In reality, this individualism of liberal theology is a typically modern accentuation: in the perspective of biblical tradition and on the horizon of Judaism, where the work of Jesus is situated in all its novelty, it is clear that the entire mission of the Son-made-flesh has a communitarian finality.

He truly came to unite dispersed humanity; he truly came to unite the People of God.

An evident sign of the intention of the Nazarene to gather together the community of the Covenant, to demonstrate in it the fulfillment of the promises made to the Fathers, who always speak of convocation, unification, unity, is *the institution of the Twelve*. We heard about this institution of the Twelve in the Gospel reading. I shall read the central passage again: "And he went up into the hills and called to him those whom he desired; and they came to him. And he appointed twelve to be with him, and to be sent out to preach and have authority to cast out demons. The names of the twelve Apostles are these . . ." (Mk 3:13–16; cf. Mt 10:1–4; Lk 6:12–16).

On the site of the revelation, "the mount", taking initiative that demonstrates absolute awareness and determination, Jesus establishes the Twelve so that, together with him, they are witnesses and heralds of the coming of the Kingdom of God.

There are no doubts about the historicity of this call, not only because of the antiquity and multiplicity of witnesses, but also for the simple reason that there is also the name of Judas, the Apostle who betrayed him, notwithstanding the difficulties that this presence could have caused the new community.

The number twelve, which evidently refers to the twelve tribes of Israel, already reveals the meaning of the prophetic-symbolic action implicit in the new initiative to re-establish the holy people. As the system of the twelve tribes had long since faded out, the hope of Israel awaited their restoration as a sign of the eschatological time (as referred to at the end of the Book of Ezekiel: 37:15–19; 39:23–29; 40–48).

In choosing the Twelve, introducing them into a communion of life with himself and involving them in his mission of proclaiming the Kingdom in words and works (cf. Mk 6:7–13; Mt 10:5–8; Lk 9:1–6; 6:13), Jesus wants to say that the definitive time has arrived in which to constitute the new People of God, the people of the twelve tribes, which now becomes a universal people, his Church.

Appeal for Israel

With their very own existence, the Twelve—called from different backgrounds—become an appeal for all of Israel to convert and allow herself to be gathered into the new covenant, complete and perfect fulfillment of the ancient one. The fact that he entrusted to his Apostles, during the Last Supper and before his Passion, the duty to celebrate his Pasch demonstrates how Jesus wished to transfer to the entire community, in the person of its heads, the mandate to be a sign and instrument in history of the eschatological gathering begun by him. In a certain sense we can say that the Last Supper itself is the act of foundation of the Church, because he gives himself and thus creates a new community, a community united in communion with himself.

In this light, one understands how the Risen One confers upon them, with the effusion of the Spirit, the power to forgive sins (cf. Jn 20:23). Thus, the Twelve Apostles are the most evident sign of Jesus' will regarding the existence and mission of his Church, the guarantee that between Christ and the Church there is no opposition: despite the sins of the people who make up the Church, they are inseparable.

Therefore, a slogan that was popular some years back: "Jesus yes, Church no", is totally irreconcilable with the intention of Christ. This individualistically chosen Jesus is an imaginary Jesus.

We cannot have Jesus without the reality he created and in

which he communicates himself. Between the Son of God-made-flesh and his Church there is a profound, unbreakable, and mysterious continuity by which Christ is present today in his people. He is always contemporary with us; he is always contemporary with the Church, built on the foundation of the Apostles and alive in the succession of the Apostles. And his very presence in the community, in which he himself is always with us, is the reason for our joy. Yes, Christ is with us; the Kingdom of God is coming.

2

"Witnesses of Christ"

WEDNESDAY, 22 MARCH 2006

Dear Brothers and Sisters,

The Letter to the Ephesians presents the Church to us as a structure built "upon the foundation of the apostles and prophets, Christ Jesus himself being the cornerstone" (Eph 2:20). In the Book of Revelation the role of the Apostles, and, more specifically, of the Twelve, is explained in the eschatological perspective of the heavenly Jerusalem, presented as a city whose walls "had twelve foundations, and on them the twelve names of the Twelve Apostles of the Lamb" (21:14).

The Gospels agree in mentioning that the call of the Apostles marked the first steps of Jesus' ministry, after the baptism he received from John the Baptist in the waters of the Jordan.

According to the accounts of Mark (1:16–20) and of Matthew (4:18–22), the scene of the call of the first Apostles is the Sea of Galilee. Jesus had just begun to preach about the Kingdom of God when his gaze came to rest upon two sets of brothers: Simon and Andrew, and James and John. They were fishermen busy with their daily work, casting their nets and mending them.

But it was another sort of fishing that awaited them. Jesus purposefully called them, and they promptly followed him: subsequently, they were to become "fishers of men" (cf. Mk

1:17; Mt 4:19). Luke, while following the same tradition, gave a more elaborate account (5:1–11).

Luke's account illustrates the development of the first disciples' faith, explaining that Jesus' invitation to follow him came after they had heard his first preaching and had seen the first miraculous signs that he worked. The miraculous catch in particular was the immediate context, and it gave its symbol to the mission of fishers of men that was entrusted to them. The destiny of those who were "called" would henceforth be closely bound to that of Jesus. An apostle is one who is sent, but even before that he is an "expert" on Jesus.

This very aspect is highlighted by the Evangelist John from Jesus' very first encounter with the future Apostles. Here the scene is different. The meeting takes place on the banks of the Jordan. The presence of the future disciples, who, like Jesus, also came from Galilee to receive the baptism administered by John, sheds light on their spiritual world.

They were men who were waiting for the Kingdom of God, anxious to know the Messiah whose coming had been proclaimed as imminent. It was enough for John the Baptist to point out Jesus to them as the Lamb of God (cf. Jn 1:36) to inspire in them the desire for a personal encounter with the Teacher.

The lines of Jesus' conversation with the first two future Apostles are most expressive. To his question "What do you seek?", they replied with another question: "'Rabbi' (which means Teacher), where are you staying?" Jesus' answer was an invitation: "Come and see" (cf. Jn 1:38–39). Come, so that you will be able to see.

This is how the Apostles' adventure began, as an encounter of people who are open to one another. For the disciples, it was the beginning of a direct acquaintance with the Teacher, seeing where he was staying and starting to get to know him.

Indeed, they were not to proclaim an idea, but to witness to a person.

Before being sent out to preach, they had to "be" with Jesus (cf. Mk 3:14), establishing a personal relationship with him. On this basis, evangelization was to be no more than the proclamation of what they felt and an invitation to enter into the mystery of communion with Christ (cf. 1 Jn 1:1–3).

To whom would the Apostles be sent? In the Gospel Jesus seemed to limit his mission to Israel alone: "I was sent only to the lost sheep of Israel" (Mt 15:24). In a similar way he seemed to restrict the mission entrusted to the Twelve: "These Twelve Jesus sent out, charging them: 'Go nowhere among the Gentiles, and enter no town of the Samaritans, but go rather to the lost sheep of the house of Israel'" (Mt 10:5ff.).

A certain rationally inspired modern criticism saw these words as showing a lack of universal awareness by the Nazarene. Actually, they should be understood in the light of his special relationship with Israel, the community of the Covenant, in continuity with the history of salvation.

According to the Messianic expectation, the divine promises directly addressed to Israel would reach fulfillment when God himself had gathered his people through his Chosen One as a shepherd gathers his flock: "I will save my flock, they shall no longer be a prey. . . . I will set up over them one shepherd, my servant David, and he shall feed them; he shall feed them and be their shepherd. And I, the Lord, shall be their God, and my servant David will be prince among them" (Ez 34:22–24).

Jesus is the eschatological shepherd who gathers the lost sheep of the house of Israel and goes in search of them because he knows and loves them (cf. Lk 15:4–7; Mt 18:12–14; cf. also the figure of the Good Shepherd in Jn 10:11ff.).

Through this "gathering together", the Kingdom of God is proclaimed to all peoples: "I will set my glory among the nations; and all the nations shall see my judgment which I have executed, and my hand which I have laid on them" (Ez 39:21). And Jesus followed precisely this prophetic indication. His first step was to "gather together" the people of Israel, so that all the people called to gather in communion with the Lord might see and believe.

Thus, the Twelve, taken on to share in the same mission as Jesus, cooperate with the Pastor of the last times, also seeking out the lost sheep of the house of Israel, that is, addressing the people of the promise whose reunion is the sign of salvation for all peoples, the beginning of the universalization of the Covenant.

Far from belying the universal openness of the Nazarene's Messianic action, the initial restriction to Israel of his mission and of the Twelve thus becomes an even more effective prophetic sign. After Christ's Passion and Resurrection, this sign was to be made clear: the universal character of the Apostles' mission was to become explicit. Christ would send the Apostles "to the whole creation" (Mk 16:15), to "all nations" (Mt 28:19; Lk 24:47), "to the ends of the earth" (Acts 1:8).

And this mission continues. The Lord's command to gather the peoples together in the unity of his love still continues. This is our hope and also our mandate: to contribute to this universality, to this true unity in the riches of cultures, in communion with our true Lord Jesus Christ.

3

The Gift of "Communion"

WEDNESDAY, 29 MARCH 2006

Dear Brothers and Sisters,

Through her apostolic ministry the Church, a community gathered by the Son of God who came in the flesh, will live on through the passing times, building up and nourishing the communion in Christ and in the Holy Spirit to which all are called and in which they can experience the salvation given by the Father.

The Twelve—as Pope Clement, the third Successor of Peter, said at the end of the first century—took pains, in fact, to prepare successors (cf. *1 Clem*, 42:4), so that the mission entrusted to them would be continued after their death. The Church, organically structured under the guidance of her legitimate Pastors, has thus continued down the ages to live in the world as a mystery of communion in which, to a certain extent, the Trinitarian Communion itself is mirrored.

The Apostle Paul was already referring to this supreme Trinitarian source when he wished his Christians: "The grace of the Lord Jesus Christ and the love of God and the fellowship of the Holy Spirit be with you all" (2 Cor 13:14).

These words, probably echoed in the worship of the newborn Church, emphasize how the free gift of the Father in Jesus Christ is realized and expressed in the communion brought about by the Holy Spirit.

This interpretation, based on the close parallelism between the three genitives that the text establishes: ("the grace *of the* Lord Jesus Christ . . . the love *of* God . . . and the fellowship *of the* Holy Spirit), presents "fellowship" as a specific gift of the Spirit, the fruit of the love given by God the Father, and the grace offered by the Lord Jesus.

Moreover, the immediate context, marked by the insistence on fraternal communion, guides us to perceiving the *koinonía* of the Holy Spirit not only as "participation" in the divine life more or less singularly, each one individually, but also, logically, as the "communion" among believers that the Spirit himself kindles as his builder and principal agent (cf. Phil 2:1).

One might say that grace, love, and communion, referring respectively to Christ, to the Father, and to the Holy Spirit, are different aspects of the one divine action for our salvation. This action creates the Church and makes the Church—as Saint Cyprian said in the third century—"a people brought into unity from the unity of the Father, the Son, and the Holy Spirit" (*De Orat. Dom.*, 23; *PL* 4, 553, cit. in *Lumen Gentium*, no. 4).

The idea of communion as participation in Trinitarian life is illuminated with special intensity in John's Gospel.

Here, the communion of love that binds the Son to the Father and to men and women is at the same time the model and source of the fraternal communion that must unite disciples with one another: "Love one another *as* I have loved you" (Jn 15:12; cf. 13:34); "that they may all be one . . . even *as* we are one" (Jn 17:21–22). Hence, it is communion of men and women with the Trinitarian God and communion of men and women with one another.

During the time of his earthly pilgrimage, the disciple can already share through communion with the Son in his divine life and that of the Father: "our fellowship is with the Father and with his Son Jesus Christ" (1 Jn 1:3).

This life of fellowship with God and with one another is the proper goal of Gospel proclamation, the goal of conversion to Christianity: "That which we have seen and heard we proclaim also to you, so that you may have fellowship with us" (1 Jn 1:2).

Thus, this twofold communion with God and with one another is inseparable. Wherever communion with God, which is communion with the Father, the Son, and the Holy Spirit, is destroyed, the root and source of our communion with one another are destroyed. And wherever we do not live communion among ourselves, communion with the Trinitarian God is not alive and true either, as we have heard.

Let us now go a step further. Communion, a fruit of the Holy Spirit, is nourished by the Eucharistic Bread (cf. 1 Cor 10:16–17) and is expressed in fraternal relations in a sort of anticipation of the future world.

In the Eucharist, Jesus nourishes us, he unites us with himself, with his Father, with the Holy Spirit, and with one another. This network of unity that embraces the world is an anticipation of the future world in our time.

Precisely in this way, since it is an anticipation of the future world, communion is also a gift with very real consequences. It lifts us from our loneliness, from being closed in on ourselves, and makes us sharers in the love that unites us to God and to one another.

It is easy to understand how great this gift is if we only think of the fragmentation and conflicts that afflict relations between individuals, groups, and entire peoples. And if the gift of unity in the Holy Spirit does not exist, the fragmentation of humanity is inevitable.

"Communion" is truly the Good News, the remedy given

to us by the Lord to fight the loneliness that threatens everyone today, the precious gift that makes us feel welcomed and beloved by God, in the unity of his People gathered in the name of the Trinity; it is the light that makes the Church shine forth like a beacon raised among the peoples.

"If we say we have fellowship with him while we walk in darkness, we lie and do not live according to the truth; but if we walk in the light, as he is in the light, we have fellowship with one another" (1 Jn 1:6ff.).

Thus, the Church, despite all the human frailties that mark her historical profile, is revealed as a marvelous creation of love, brought into being to bring Christ close to every man and every woman who truly desires to meet him, until the end of time. And in the Church, the Lord always remains our contemporary. Scripture is not something of the past. The Lord does not speak in the past but speaks in the present, he speaks to us today, he enlightens us, he shows us the way through life, he gives us communion and thus he prepares us and opens us to peace.

4

"Safeguarding the Gift"

WEDNESDAY, 5 APRIL 2006

Dear Brothers and Sisters,

In the new series of Catecheses that began a few weeks ago, we are considering the origins of the Church so as to understand Jesus' original plan and thereby grasp the essential of the Church that lives on through the changing times. Thus, we also understand the reason for our being in the Church and how we must strive to live it at the dawn of a new Christian millennium.

In thinking about the newborn Church, we can discover two aspects: a first aspect is strongly highlighted by Saint Irenaeus of Lyons, a martyr and great theologian of the end of the second century, the first to have given us a theology that was to a certain extent systematic. Saint Irenaeus wrote: "Wherever the Church is, God's Spirit is too; and wherever God's Spirit is, there is the Church and every grace; for the Spirit is truth" (*Adversus Haereses*, III, 24, 1: *PG* 7, 966).

Thus, a deep bond exists between the Holy Spirit and the Church. The Holy Spirit builds the Church and gives her the truth; he pours out love, as Saint Paul says, into the hearts of believers (cf. Rom 5:5).

Then there is a second aspect. This deep bond with the Spirit does not eradicate our humanity, with all of its weaknesses. So it is that from the start the community of the disciples has known not only the joy of the Holy Spirit, the grace of truth and love, but also trials that are constituted above all by disagreements about the truths of faith, with the consequent wounds to communion.

Just as the fellowship of love has existed since the outset and will continue to the end (cf. 1 Jn 1:1ff.), so also, from the start, division unfortunately arose. We should not be surprised that it still exists today. "They went out from us, but they were not of us", John says in his First Letter, "for if they had been of us, they would have continued with us; but they went out, that it might be plain that they are not of us" (1 Jn 2:19).

Thus, in the events of the world but also in the weaknesses of the Church, there is always a risk of losing faith, hence, also love and brotherhood. Consequently, it is a specific duty of those who believe in the Church of love and want to live in her to recognize this danger too and accept that communion is no longer possible with those who have drifted away from the doctrine of salvation (cf. 2 Jn 9–11).

That the newborn Church was well aware of the possible tensions in the experience of communion is clearly shown by John's First Letter: no voice is more forcefully raised in the New Testament to highlight the reality and duty of fraternal love among Christians; but the same voice is addressed with drastic severity to adversaries of the Church who used to be members of the community but now no longer belong to it.

The Church of love is also the Church of truth, understood primarily as fidelity to the Gospel entrusted by the Lord Jesus to his followers. It was being made children of the same Father by the Spirit of truth that gave rise to Christian brotherhood: "For all who are led by the Spirit of God are sons of God" (Rom 8:14).

However, if the family of God's children is to live in unity and peace, it needs someone to keep it in the truth and guide it with wise and authoritative discernment: this is what the ministry of the Apostles is required to do.

And here we come to an important point. The Church is wholly of the Spirit but has a structure, the apostolic succession, which is responsible for guaranteeing that the Church endures in the truth given by Christ, from whom the capacity to love also comes.

The first brief description in the Acts sums up very effectively the convergence of these values in the life of the newborn Church: "And they devoted themselves to the Apostles' teaching and fellowship (*koinonía*), to the breaking of bread and the prayers" (Acts 2:42). Communion is born from faith inspired by apostolic preaching, it is nourished by the Breaking of Bread and prayer and is expressed in brotherly love and service.

We have before us the description of fellowship in the newborn Church with the riches of its internal dynamism and visible expressions: the gift of communion is safeguarded and promoted in particular by the apostolic ministry, which in turn is a gift for the entire community.

The Apostles and their successors are therefore the custodians and authoritative witnesses of the deposit of truth consigned to the Church and are likewise the ministers of charity. These are two aspects that go together.

They must always be mindful of the inseparable nature of this twofold service which in fact is only one: truth and love, revealed and given by the Lord Jesus. In this regard, their service is first and foremost a service of love: and the charity they live and foster is inseparable from the truth they preserve and pass on.

Truth and love are the two faces of the same gift that comes from God and, thanks to the apostolic ministry, is safeguarded in the Church and handed down to us, to our present time!

And the love of the Trinitarian God also reaches us through the service of the Apostles and their successors, to communicate to us the truth that sets us free (cf. Jn 8:32)!

All this, which we see in the newborn Church, impels us to pray for the Successors of the Apostles, for all the Bishops and for the Successors of Peter, so that together they may truly be at the same time custodians of truth and love; so that, in this regard, they may truly be apostles of Christ and that his light, the light of truth and love, may never be extinguished in the Church or in the world.

5

Communion in Time: Tradition

Dear Brothers and Sisters,

Thank you for your affection! In the new series of Catecheses, recently begun, we are seeking to understand the original plan of the Church which the Lord desired, in order to understand better our place, our Christian life, in the great communion of the Church.

So far we have understood that ecclesial communion is inspired and sustained by the Holy Spirit and preserved and promoted by the apostolic ministry. And this communion, which we call "Church", does not only extend to all believers in a specific historical period, but also embraces all the epochs and all the generations. Thus, we have a twofold universality: a synchronic universality—we are united with believers in every part of the world—and also a so-called diachronic universality, that is: all the epochs belong to us, and all the believers of the past and of the future form with us a single great communion.

The Holy Spirit appears to us as the guarantor of the active presence of the mystery in history, the One who ensures its realization down the centuries. Thanks to the Paraclete, it will always be possible for subsequent generations to have the same experience of the Risen One that was lived by the apostolic community at the origin of the Church, since it is passed on and actualized in the faith, worship, and communion of the People of God, on pilgrim-age through time.

And so it is that we today, in the Easter Season, are living the encounter with the Risen One not only as something of the past, but in the present communion of the faith, liturgy, and life of the Church. The Church's apostolic Tradition consists in this transmission of the goods of salvation which, through the power of the Spirit, makes the Christian com-munity the permanent actualization of the original com-munion.

It is called "original" because it was born of the witness of the Apostles and of the community of the disciples at the time of the origins. It was passed on under the guidance of the Holy Spirit in the New Testament writings and in the sacramental life, in the life of the faith, and the Church continuously refers to it—to this Tradition, which is the whole, ever up-to-date reality of Jesus' gift—as her founda-tion and her law, through the uninterrupted succession of the apostolic ministry.

In his historical life, furthermore, Jesus limited his mission to the house of Israel but already made it clear that the gift was not only destined for the People of Israel but to everyone in the world and to every epoch.

The Risen One then explicitly entrusted to the Apostles (cf. Lk 6:13) the task of making disciples of all the nations, guaranteeing his presence and help to the end of the age (cf. Mt 28:19ff.).

The universalism of salvation, moreover, requires that the Easter memorial be celebrated in history without interrup-tion until Christ's glorious return (cf. 1 Cor 11:26). Who will bring about the saving presence of the Lord Jesus through the ministry of the Apostles—heads of the eschatological Israel (cf. Mt 19:28)—and through the whole life of the people of the New Covenant? The answer is clear: the Holy Spirit. The Acts of the Apostles—in continuity with the pattern of Luke's Gospel—show vividly the interpenetration between the Spirit, those sent out by Christ, and the community they have gathered.

Thanks to the action of the Paraclete, the Apostles and their successors can realize in time the mission received from the Risen One. "You are witnesses of these things. And behold, I send the promise of my Father upon you" (Lk 24:48ff.).

"You shall receive power when the Holy Spirit has come upon you; and you shall be my witnesses in Jerusalem and in all Judea and Samaria and to the end of the earth" (Acts 1:8). And this promise, which at first seems incredible, already came true in the Apostles' time: "And we are witnesses to these things, and so is the Holy Spirit whom God has given to those who obey him" (Acts 5:32).

So it is the Spirit himself who, through the laying on of hands and prayers of the Apostles, consecrates and sends out new Gospel missionaries (as, for example, in Acts 13:3ff. and 1 Tm 4:14). It is interesting to observe that whereas in some passages it says that Paul appointed elders in every Church (cf. Acts 14:23), elsewhere it says that it is the Spirit who has made them guardians of the flock (cf. Acts 20:28).

The action of the Spirit and the action of Paul thus are deeply interwoven. At the time of solemn decisions for the life of the Church, the Spirit is present to guide her. This guiding presence of the Holy Spirit was particularly acutely felt in the Council of Jerusalem, in whose conclusive words resounds the affirmation: "For it has seemed good to the Holy Spirit and to us . . ." (Acts 15:28); the Church grows and walks "in the fear of the Lord, and in the comfort of the Holy Spirit" (Acts 9:31). This permanent actualization of the active presence of the Lord Jesus in his People, brought about by the Holy Spirit and expressed in the Church through the apostolic ministry and fraternal communion, is what, in a theological sense, is meant by the term "Tradition": it is not merely the material transmission of what was given at the beginning to the Apostles, but the effective presence of the Crucified and Risen Lord Jesus, who accompanies and guides in the Spirit the community he has gathered together.

Tradition is the communion of the faithful around their legitimate Pastors down through history, a communion that the Holy Spirit nurtures, assuring the connection between the experience of the apostolic faith, lived in the original community of the disciples, and the actual experience of Christ in his Church.

In other words, Tradition is the practical continuity of the Church, the holy Temple of God the Father, built on the foundation of the Apostles and held together by the cornerstone, Christ, through the life-giving action of the Spirit: "So then you are no longer strangers and sojourners, but you are fellow citizens with the saints and members of the household of God, built upon the foundation of the apostles and prophets, Christ Jesus himself being the cornerstone, in whom the whole structure is joined together and grows into a holy temple in the Lord; in whom you also are built into it for a dwelling place of God in the Spirit" (Eph 2:19–22).

Thanks to Tradition, guaranteed by the ministry of the Apostles and by their successors, the water of life that flowed from Christ's side and his saving blood reach the women and men of all times. Thus, Tradition is the permanent presence of the Savior who comes to meet us, to redeem us, and to sanctify us in the Spirit, through the ministry of his Church, to the glory of the Father.

Concluding and summing up, we can therefore say that

Tradition is not the transmission of things or words, a collection of dead things. Tradition is the living river that links us to the origins, the living river in which the origins are ever present, the great river that leads us to the gates of eternity. And since this is so, in this living river the words of the Lord that we heard on the reader's lips to start with are ceaselessly brought about: "I am with you always, to the close of the age" (Mt 28:20).

6

The Apostolic Tradition of the Church

Dear Brothers and Sisters,

In these Catecheses we wish to understand a little more what the Church is. The last time we meditated on the theme of apostolic Tradition. We saw that it is not a collection of things or words, like a box of dead things. Tradition is the river of new life that flows from the origins, from Christ down to us, and makes us participate in God's history with humanity.

This topic of Tradition is so important that I would like to reflect upon it again today: indeed, it is of great importance for the life of the Church.

The Second Vatican Council pointed out in this regard that Tradition is primarily *apostolic* in its origins: "God graciously arranged that the things he had once revealed for the salvation of all peoples should remain in their entirety, throughout the ages, and be transmitted to all generations. Therefore, Christ the Lord, in whom the entire Revelation of the Most High God is summed up (cf. 2 Cor 1:20 and 3:16, 4:6), commanded the Apostles to preach the Gospel . . . and communicate the gifts of God to all men. This Gospel was to be the source of all saving truth and moral discipline" (Dogmatic Constitution on Divine Revelation *Dei Verbum*, no. 7).

The Council noted further that this was faithfully done

"by the Apostles who handed on, by the spoken word of
their preaching, by the example they gave, by the institutions
they established, what they themselves had received—
whether from the lips of Christ, from his way of life and his
works, or whether they had learned it at the prompting of the
Holy Spirit" (*ibid.*).

The Council adds that there were "other men associated
with the Apostles, who, under the inspiration of the same
Holy Spirit, committed the message of salvation to writing"
(*ibid.*).

As heads of the eschatological Israel, and likewise as
Twelve, the number of the tribes of the Chosen People, the
Apostles continued the "gathering" begun by the Lord and
did so first and foremost by transmitting faithfully the gift
received, the Good News of the Kingdom that came to
people in Jesus Christ.

Their number not only expresses continuity with the holy
root, the Israel of the twelve tribes, but also the universal
destination of their ministry, which brought salvation to the
very ends of the earth.

This can be understood from the symbolic value that the
numbers have in the Semitic world: *twelve* results from the
multiplication of three, a perfect number, and *four*, a number
that refers to the four cardinal points, hence, to the whole
world.

The community, born from the proclamation of the Gospel, recognizes that it was called by the words of those who
were the first to experience the Lord and were sent out by
him. It knows that it can count on the guidance of the
Twelve, as well as that of those who were gradually associated
with them as their successors in the ministry of the Word and
in the service of communion. Consequently, the community
feels committed to transmit to others the "Good News" of

the actual presence of the Lord and of his Paschal Mystery, brought about in the Spirit.

This is clearly highlighted and visible in certain passages of the Pauline Letters: "I delivered to you . . . what I also received" (1 Cor 15:3). And this is important. Saint Paul, it is well known, originally called by Christ with a personal vocation, was a real Apostle, yet for him too, fidelity to what he received was fundamentally important. He did not want "to invent" a new, so-to-speak, "Pauline" Christianity. Therefore, he insisted, "I have passed on to you what I too received." He passed on the initial gift that comes from the Lord and the truth that saves.

Then, towards the end of his life, he wrote to Timothy: "Guard this rich trust with the help of the Holy Spirit that dwells within us" (2 Tm 1:14).

It is also effectively demonstrated by this ancient testimony of the Christian faith written by Tertullian in about the year 200: "[The Apostles] after first bearing witness to the faith in Jesus Christ throughout Judea and founding Churches [there], they next went forth into the world and preached the same doctrine of the same faith to the nations. They then in like manner founded Churches in every city, from which all the other Churches, one after another, derived the tradition of the faith and the seeds of doctrine, and are every day deriving them, that they may become Churches. Indeed, it is on this account only that they will be able to deem themselves apostolic, as being the offspring of apostolic Churches" (Tertullian, *De Praescriptione Haereticorum*, 20: *PL* 2, 32).

The Second Vatican Council comments: "What was handed on by the Apostles comprises everything that serves to make the People of God live their lives in holiness and increase their faith. In this way the Church, in her doctrine,

life, and worship, perpetuates and transmits to every generation all that she herself is, all that she believes" (*Dei Verbum*,
no. 8).

The Church transmits all that she is and believes; she hands
it down through worship, life, and doctrine.

So it is that Tradition is the living Gospel, proclaimed by
the Apostles in its integrity on the basis of the fullness of
their unique and unrepeatable experience: through their
activity the faith is communicated to others, even down to
us, until the end of the world. Tradition, therefore, is the
history of the Spirit who acts in the Church's history
through the mediation of the Apostles and their successors,
in faithful continuity with the experience of the origins.

This is what Saint Clement of Rome said towards the end
of the first century:

> The Apostles [he wrote] have preached the Gospel to us from
> the Lord Jesus Christ; Jesus Christ was sent by God. Christ,
> therefore, was sent forth by God, and the Apostles by Christ.
>
> Both these appointments, then, were made in an orderly
> way, according to the will of God. . . . Our Apostles also
> knew, through Our Lord Jesus Christ, that there would be
> strife on account of the episcopal office.
>
> For this reason, therefore, inasmuch as they had obtained
> a perfect foreknowledge of this, they appointed those [min-
> isters] already mentioned, and afterwards gave instructions
> that when these should fall asleep, other approved men
> should succeed them in their ministry. (*Ad Corinthios*, 42, 44:
> *PG* 1, 292, 296)

This chain of service has continued until today; it will
continue to the end of the world. Indeed, the mandate that
Jesus conferred upon the Apostles was passed on by them to
their successors. Going beyond the experience of personal
contact with Christ, unique and unrepeatable, the Apostles

passed on to their successors the solemn mandate that they had received from the Master to go out into the world. "Apostle" comes precisely from the Greek term *apostéllein*, which means "to send forth".

The apostolic mandate—as the text of Matthew shows (Mt 28:19ff.)—implies a service that is pastoral ("Go therefore and make disciples of all the nations . . ."), liturgical ("baptizing them"), and prophetic ("teaching them to observe all that I have commanded you"), guaranteed by the Lord's closeness, until the end of time ("and lo, I am with you always, to the close of the age").

Thus, but differently from the Apostles, we too have a true, personal experience of the presence of the Risen Lord.

Therefore, through the apostolic ministry it is Christ himself who reaches those who are called to the faith. The distance of the centuries is overcome, and the Risen One offers himself alive and active for our sake, in the Church and in the world today.

This is our great joy. In the living river of Tradition, Christ is not two thousand years away but is really present among us and gives us the Truth, he gives us the light that makes us live and find the way towards the future.

7

Having a "Vision from on High"

Dear Brothers and Sisters,

At the last two Audiences we meditated on what Tradition in the Church is, and we saw that it is the permanent presence of the word and life of Jesus among his people. But in order to be present, the word needs a person, a witness.

And so it is that this reciprocity comes about: on the one hand, the word needs the person, but on the other, the person, the witness, is bound to the word, entrusted to him and not invented by him. This reciprocity between the content—the Word of God, life of the Lord—and the person who carries on the work is characteristic of the Church's structure. Let us meditate today on this personal aspect of the Church.

The Lord founded the Church, as we have seen, by calling together the Twelve, who were to represent the future People of God. Faithful to the Lord's mandate, after his Ascension, the Twelve first made up their number by appointing Matthias in Judas' place (cf. Acts 1:15–26), thereby continuing to involve others in the duties entrusted to them so that they might continue their ministry.

The Risen Lord himself called Paul (cf. Gal 1:1), but Paul, although he was called by the Lord to be an Apostle, compared his Gospel with the Gospel of the Twelve (cf. *ibid.*, 1:18) and was concerned to transmit what he had received (cf. 1 Cor 11:23; 15:3–4). In the distribution of missionary tasks, he was associated with the Apostles together with others, for example, Barnabas (cf. Gal 2:9).

Just as becoming an Apostle begins with being called and sent out by the Risen One, so the subsequent call and sending out to others was to be brought about, through the power of the Spirit, by those who are already ordained in the apostolic ministry. And this is the way in which this ministry, known from the second generation as the episcopal ministry, *episcope*, was to be continued.

Perhaps it would be useful to explain briefly what "bishop" means. It is the Italian form of the Greek term *episcopos*. This word means one who has a vision from on high, who looks with the heart. This is what Saint Peter himself calls Jesus in his First Letter: bishop, "Shepherd and Guardian of your souls" (1 Pt 2:25).

And according to this new model of the Lord, who was the first Bishop, Guardian, and Pastor of souls, the successors of the Apostles were later called Bishops, *episcopoi*. The role of "episcope" was entrusted to them. This specific role of the Bishop was gradually to evolve, in comparison with the origins, until it took the form—already clearly attested to by Ignatius of Antioch at the beginning of the second century (cf. *Ad Magnesios*, 6, 1: PG 5, 668)—of the threefold office of Bishop, Priest, and Deacon.

This development was guided by God's Spirit who helps the Church in the discernment of the authentic forms of apostolic succession, ever more clearly defined among the plurality of experiences and charismatic and ministerial forms present in the earliest communities.

In this way, succession in the role of Bishop is presented as the continuity of the apostolic ministry, a guarantee of the permanence of the apostolic Tradition, word, and life, entrusted to us by the Lord. The link between the College of Bishops and the original community of the Apostles is understood above all in the line of historical continuity.

As we have seen, first Matthias, then Paul, then Barnabas joined the Twelve, then others, until, in the second and third generations, the Bishop's ministry took shape.

Continuity, therefore, is expressed in this historical chain. And in the continuity of the succession lies the guarantee of the permanence, in the Ecclesial Community, of the Apostolic College that Christ had gathered around him.

This continuity, however, which we see first in the historical continuity of ministries, should also be understood in a spiritual sense, because apostolic succession in the ministry is considered a privileged place for the action and transmission of the Holy Spirit.

We find these convictions clearly echoed in the following text, for example, by Irenaeus of Lyons (second half of the second century): "It is within the power of all . . . in every Church, who may wish to see the truth, to contemplate clearly the tradition of the Apostles manifested throughout the whole world; and we are in a position to count those who were by the Apostles instituted Bishops in the Churches and . . . the succession of these men to our own times. . . . [The Apostles] were desirous that these men, whom also they were leaving behind as their successors, should be very perfect and blameless in all things, delivering up their own place of government to these men; which men, if they discharged their functions honestly, would be a great boon, but if they should fall away, the direst calamity" (*Adversus Haereses*, III, 3, 1: *PG* 7, 848).

Pointing to this network of apostolic succession as a guarantee of the permanence of the Lord's word, Irenaeus then concentrated on that Church, "the very great, the very

ancient and universally known Church founded and orga-
nized at Rome by the two most glorious Apostles, Peter and
Paul", highlighting the Tradition of faith that in her comes
down to us from the Apostles through the succession of the
Bishops.

In this way, for Irenaeus and for the universal Church, the
episcopal succession of the Church of Rome becomes the
sign, criterion, and guarantee of the unbroken transmission
of apostolic faith: "For it is a matter of necessity that every
Church should agree with this Church, on account of her
pre-eminent authority (*propter potiorem principalitatem*)—that
is, the faithful everywhere—inasmuch as the apostolic Tradition has been preserved continuously . . ." (*ibid.*, III, 3, 2:
PG 7, 848).

Apostolic succession, verified on the basis of communion
with that of the Church of Rome, is therefore the criterion
of the permanence of the particular Churches in the Tradition of the common apostolic faith, which from the origins
has come down to us through this channel: "In this order,
and by this succession, the ecclesiastical Tradition from the
Apostles and the preaching of the truth have come down to
us. And this is a most abundant proof that there is one and the
same vivifying faith, which has been preserved in the Church
from the Apostles until now and handed down in truth"
(*ibid.*, III, 3, 3: *PG* 7, 851).

According to this testimony of the ancient Church, the
apostolicity of ecclesial communion consists in fidelity to
the teaching and praxis of the Apostles, through whom
the historical and spiritual bond of the Church with Christ
is assured. The apostolic succession of the episcopal ministry
is a means of guaranteeing the faithful transmission of the
apostolic witness.

What the Apostles represent in the relationship between

the Lord Jesus and the Church of the origins is similarly represented by the ministerial succession in the relationship between the primitive Church and the Church of today. It is not merely a material sequence; rather, it is a historical instrument that the Spirit uses to make the Lord Jesus, Head of his people, present through those who are ordained for the ministry through the imposition of hands and the Bishops' prayer.

Consequently, through apostolic succession it is Christ who reaches us: in the words of the Apostles and of their successors, it is he who speaks to us; through their hands it is he who acts in the sacraments; in their gaze it is his gaze that embraces us and makes us feel loved and welcomed into the Heart of God. And still today, as at the outset, Christ himself is the true Shepherd and Guardian of our souls whom we follow with deep trust, gratitude, and joy.

8

Peter, the Fisherman

WEDNESDAY, 17 MAY 2006

Dear Brothers and Sisters,

In the new series of Catecheses, we have tried above all to understand better what the Church is and what idea the Lord has about this new family of his. Then we said that the Church exists in people, and we have seen that the Lord entrusted this new reality, the Church, to the Twelve Apostles. Let us now look at them one by one, to understand through these people what it means to experience the Church and what it means to follow Jesus. We begin with Saint Peter.

After Jesus, Peter is the figure best known and most frequently cited in the New Testament writings: he is mentioned 154 times with the nickname of *Pétros*, "rock", which is the Greek translation of the Aramaic name Jesus gave him directly: *Cephas*, attested to nine times, especially in Paul's Letters; then the frequently occurring name *Simon* (75 times) must be added; this is a hellenization of his original Hebrew name *Symeon* (twice: Acts 15:14; 2 Pt 1:1).

Son of John (cf. Jn 1:42) or, in the Aramaic form, "Bar-Jona, son of Jona" (cf. Mt 16:17), Simon was from Bethsaida (cf. Jn 1:44), a little town to the east of the Sea of Galilee, from which Philip also came and, of course, Andrew, the brother of Simon.

He spoke with a Galilean accent. Like his brother, he too

was a fisherman: with the family of Zebedee, the father of James and John, he ran a small fishing business on the Lake of Gennesaret (cf. Lk 5:10). Thus, he must have been reasonably well-off and was motivated by a sincere interest in religion, by a desire for God—he wanted God to intervene in the world—a desire that impelled him to go with his brother as far as Judea to hear the preaching of John the Baptist (Jn 1:35–42).

He was a believing and practicing Jew who trusted in the active presence of God in his people's history and grieved not to see God's powerful action in the events he was witnessing at that time. He was married, and his mother-in-law, whom Jesus was one day to heal, lived in the city of Capernaum, in the house where Simon also stayed when he was in that town (cf. Mt 8:14ff.; Mk 1:29ff.; Lk 4:38ff.).

Recent archaeological excavations have brought to light, beneath the octagonal mosaic paving of a small Byzantine church, the remains of a more ancient church built in that house, as the graffiti with invocations to Peter testify.

The Gospels tell us that Peter was one of the first four disciples of the Nazarene (cf. Lk 5:1–11), to whom a fifth was added, complying with the custom of every rabbi to have five disciples (cf. Lk 5:27: called Levi). When Jesus went from five disciples to twelve (cf. Lk 9:1–6), the newness of his mission became evident: he was not one of the numerous rabbis but had come to gather together the eschatological Israel, symbolized by the number twelve, the number of the tribes of Israel.

Simon appears in the Gospels with a determined and impulsive character: he is ready to assert his own opinions even with force (remember him using the sword in the Garden of Olives: cf. Jn 18:10ff.). At the same time he is also ingenuous and fearful, yet he is honest, to the point of the most sincere repentance (cf. Mt 26:75).

The Gospels enable us to follow Peter step by step on his spiritual journey. The starting point was Jesus' call. It happened on an ordinary day while Peter was busy with his fisherman's tasks. Jesus was at the Lake of Gennesaret, and crowds had gathered around him to listen to him. The size of his audience created a certain discomfort. The Teacher saw two boats moored by the shore; the fishermen had disembarked and were washing their nets. He then asked permission to board the boat, which was Simon's, and requested him to put out a little from the land. Sitting on that improvised seat, he began to teach the crowds from the boat (cf. Lk 5:1–3). Thus, the boat of Peter becomes the chair of Jesus.

When he had finished speaking he said to Simon: "Put out into the deep and let down your nets for a catch." And Simon answered, "Master, we toiled all night and took nothing! But at your word I will let down the nets" (Lk 5:4–5). Jesus, a carpenter, was not a skilled fisherman: yet Simon the fisherman trusted this Rabbi, who did not give him answers but required him to trust him.

His reaction to the miraculous catch showed his amazement and fear: "Depart from me, for I am a sinful man, O Lord" (Lk 5:8). Jesus replied by inviting him to trust and to be open to a project that would surpass all his expectations. "Do not be afraid; henceforth, you will be catching men" (Lk 5:10). Peter could not yet imagine that one day he would arrive in Rome and that here he would be a "fisher of men" for the Lord. He accepted this surprising call; he let himself be involved in this great adventure: he was generous; he recognized his limits but believed in the one who was calling him and followed the dream of his heart. He said "yes", a courageous and generous "yes", and became a disciple of Jesus.

Peter was to live another important moment of his spiritual journey near Caesarea Philippi when Jesus asked the disciples a precise question: "Who do men say that I am?" (Mk 8:27). But for Jesus hearsay did not suffice. He wanted from those who had agreed to be personally involved with him a personal statement of their position. Consequently, he insisted: "But who do you say that I am?" (Mk 8:29).

It was Peter who answered on behalf of the others: "You are the Christ" (*ibid.*), that is, the Messiah. Peter's answer, which was not revealed to him by "flesh and blood" but was given to him by the Father who is in heaven (cf. Mt 16:17), contains as in a seed the future confession of faith of the Church. However, Peter had not yet understood the profound content of Jesus' Messianic mission, the new meaning of this word: Messiah.

He demonstrates this a little later, inferring that the Messiah whom he is following in his dreams is very different from God's true plan. He was shocked by the Lord's announcement of the Passion and protested, prompting a lively reaction from Jesus (cf. Mk 8:32–33).

Peter wanted as Messiah a "divine man" who would fulfill the expectations of the people by imposing his power upon them all: we would also like the Lord to impose his power and transform the world instantly. Jesus presented himself as a "human God", the Servant of God, who turned the crowd's expectations upside-down by taking a path of humility and suffering.

This is the great alternative that we must learn over and over again: to give priority to our own expectations, rejecting Jesus, or to accept Jesus in the truth of his mission and set aside all too human expectations.

Peter, impulsive as he was, did not hesitate to take Jesus aside and rebuke him. Jesus' answer demolished all his false expectations, calling him to conversion and to follow him: "Get behind me, Satan! For you are not on the side of God, but of men" (Mk 8:33). It is not for you to show me the way; I take my own way and you should follow me.

Peter thus learned what following Jesus truly means. It was his second call, similar to Abraham's in Genesis 22, after that in Genesis 12: "If any man would come after me, let him deny himself and take up his cross and follow me. For whoever would save his life will lose it; and whoever loses his life for my sake and the Gospel's will save it" (Mk 8:34–35). This is the demanding rule of the following of Christ: one must be able, if necessary, to give up the whole world to save the true values, to save the soul, to save the presence of God in the world (cf. Mk 8:36–37). And though with difficulty, Peter accepted the invitation and continued his life in the Master's footsteps.

And it seems to me that these conversions of Saint Peter on different occasions, and his whole figure, are a great consolation and a great lesson for us. We too have a desire for God; we too want to be generous, but we too expect God to be strong in the world and to transform the world on the spot, according to our ideas and the needs that we perceive.

God chooses a different way. God chooses the way of the transformation of hearts in suffering and in humility. And we, like Peter, must convert, over and over again. We must follow Jesus and not go before him: it is he who shows us the way.

So it is that Peter tells us: You think you have the recipe and that it is up to you to transform Christianity, but it is the Lord who knows the way. It is the Lord who says to me, who says to you: Follow me! And we must have the courage and humility to follow Jesus, because he is the Way, the Truth, and the Life.

9

Peter, the Apostle

WEDNESDAY, 24 MAY 2006

Dear Brothers and Sisters,

In these Catecheses, we are meditating on the Church. We said that the Church lives in people and therefore, in last week's Catechesis, we began to meditate on the characters of the individual Apostles, beginning with Saint Peter.

We examined two decisive stages of his life: the call [to follow Jesus] near the Sea of Galilee, and then the confession of faith: "You are Christ, the Messiah." It is a confession, we said, that is still lacking, initial and yet open. Saint Peter puts himself on a path of "sequela", following. And so, this initial confession carries within it, like a seed, the future faith of the Church.

Today, we want to consider another two important events in the life of Saint Peter: the multiplication of the loaves—we heard the Lord's question and Saint Peter's reply in the Gospel passage just read—and then the Lord who calls Peter to be Pastor of the universal Church.

Let us now begin with the multiplication of the loaves. You know that the people had been listening to the Lord for hours. At the end, Jesus says: They are tired and hungry; we must give these people something to eat. The Apostles ask: But how? And Andrew, Peter's brother, draws Jesus' attention to a boy who has with him five loaves of bread and two fish. But what is this for so many people, the Apostles ask.

The Lord has the crowd be seated and these five loaves and two fish distributed. And the hunger of everyone is satisfied; what is more, the Lord gives the Apostles—Peter among them—the duty to collect the abundant leftovers: twelve baskets of bread (cf. Jn 6:12–13).

Afterwards, the people, seeing this miracle—that seemed to be the much-awaited renewal of a new "manna", of the gift of bread from heaven—wanted to make him king. But Jesus does not accept and withdraws into the hills by himself to pray. The following day, on the other side of the lake in the Synagogue of Capernaum, Jesus explained the miracle—not in the sense of a kingship over Israel with a worldly power in the way the crowds hoped, but in the sense of the gift of self: "The bread which I shall give for the life of the world is my flesh" (Jn 6:51).

Jesus announces the Cross and with the Cross the true multiplication of the loaves, the Eucharistic bread—his absolutely new way of kingship, a way completely contrary to the expectations of the people.

We can understand that these words of the Master, who does not want to multiply bread every day, who does not want to offer Israel a worldly power, would be really difficult, indeed, unacceptable, for the people. "He gives his flesh": what does this mean?

Even for the disciples what Jesus says in this moment seems unacceptable. It was and is for our heart, for our mentality, a "hard saying" which is a trial of faith (cf. Jn 6:60). Many of the disciples went away. They wanted someone who would truly renew the State of Israel, of his people, and not one who said: "I give my flesh."

We can imagine that the words of Jesus were difficult for Peter too, who at Caesarea Philippi had protested at the prophecy of the Cross. However, when Jesus asked the

Twelve: "Will you also go away?" Peter reacted with the enthusiasm of his generous heart, guided by the Holy Spirit.

Speaking on everyone's behalf, he answered with immortal words, which are also our words: "Lord, to whom shall we go? You have the words of eternal life; and we have believed, and have come to know, that you are the Holy One of God" (cf. Jn 6:66–69).

Here, as at Caesarea, Peter begins with his words the confession of the Church's Christological faith and becomes spokesman also for the other Apostles and for us believers of all times. This does not mean that he had already understood the mystery of Christ in all its depth; his faith was still at the beginning of a journey of faith. It would reach its true fullness only through the experience of the Paschal events.

Nonetheless, it was already faith, open to the greatest reality; open especially because it was not faith in something, it was faith in Someone: in him, Christ.

And so, our faith too is always an initial one, and we have still to carry out a great journey. But it is essential that it is an open faith and that we allow ourselves to be led by Jesus, because he does not only know the Way, but he is the Way.

Peter's rash generosity does not protect him, however, from the risks connected with human weakness. Moreover, it is what we too can recognize in our own lives. Peter followed Jesus with enthusiasm; he overcame the trial of faith, abandoning himself to Christ. The moment comes, however, when he gives in to fear and falls: he betrays the Master (cf. Mk 14:66–72).

The school of faith is not a triumphal march but a journey marked daily by suffering and love, trials and faithfulness. Peter, who promised absolute fidelity, knew the bitterness and humiliation of denial: the arrogant man learns the costly lesson of humility. Peter, too, must learn that he is weak and in need of forgiveness.

Once his attitude changes and he understands the truth of his weak heart of a believing sinner, he weeps in a fit of liberating repentance. After this weeping he is finally ready for his mission.

On a spring morning, this mission will be entrusted to him by the Risen Christ. The encounter takes place on the shore of the Lake of Tiberias. John the Evangelist recounts the conversation between Jesus and Peter in that circumstance. There is a very significant play on words.

In Greek, the word *fileo* means the love of friendship, tender but not all-encompassing; instead, the word *agapao* means love without reserve, total and unconditional. Jesus asks Peter the first time: "Simon . . . do you love me (*agapas-me*)" with this total and unconditional love (Jn 21:15)?

Prior to the experience of betrayal, the Apostle certainly would have said: "I love you (*agapo-se*) unconditionally." Now that he has known the bitter sadness of infidelity, the drama of his own weakness, he says with humility: "Lord; you know that I love you (*filo-se*)", that is, "I love you with my poor human love." Christ insists: "Simon, do you love me with this total love that I want?" And Peter repeats the response of his humble human love: "*Kyrie, filo-se*", "Lord, I love you as I am able to love you." The third time Jesus only says to Simon: "*Fileis-me?*", "Do you love me?"

Simon understands that his poor love is enough for Jesus, it is the only one of which he is capable; nonetheless he is grieved that the Lord spoke to him in this way. He thus replies: "Lord, you know everything; you know that I love you (*filo-se*)."

This is to say that Jesus has put himself on the level of

Peter, rather than Peter on Jesus' level! It is exactly this divine conformity that gives hope to the Disciple, who experienced the pain of infidelity.

From here is born the trust that makes him able to follow [Christ] to the end: "This he said to show by what death he was to glorify God. And after this he said to him, 'Follow me'" (Jn 21:19).

From that day, Peter "followed" the Master with the precise awareness of his own fragility; but this understanding did not discourage him. Indeed, he knew that he could count on the presence of the Risen One beside him.

From the naïve enthusiasm of initial acceptance, passing through the sorrowful experience of denial and the weeping of conversion, Peter succeeded in entrusting himself to that Jesus who adapted himself to his poor capacity of love. And in this way he shows us the way, notwithstanding all of our weakness. We know that Jesus adapts himself to this weakness of ours.

We follow him with our poor capacity to love, and we know that Jesus is good and he accepts us.

It was a long journey for Peter that made him a trustworthy witness, "rock" of the Church, because he was constantly open to the action of the Spirit of Jesus.

Peter qualifies himself as a "witness of the sufferings of Christ as well as a partaker in the glory that is to be revealed" (1 Pt 5:1). When he wrote these words he was already elderly, heading towards the end of his life that would be sealed with martyrdom. He was then ready to describe true joy and to indicate where it could be drawn from: the source is believing in and loving Christ with our weak but sincere faith, notwithstanding our fragility.

He would therefore write to the Christians of his community, and says also to us: "Without having seen him you love him; though you do not now see him you believe in him and rejoice with unutterable and exalted joy. As the outcome of your faith you obtain the salvation of your souls" (1 Pt 1:8–9).

10

Peter, the Rock

WEDNESDAY, 7 JUNE 2006

Dear Brothers and Sisters,

We are returning to the weekly Catecheses that we began this spring. In the last Catechesis two weeks ago, I spoke of Peter as the first of the Apostles; today let us return once again to this great and important figure of the Church.

In recounting Jesus' first meeting with Simon, the brother of Andrew, John the Evangelist records a unique event: Jesus "looked at him and said, 'So you are Simon the son of John? You shall be called Cephas (which means Peter)'" (Jn 1:42).

It was not Jesus' practice to change his disciples' names: apart from the nickname "sons of thunder", which in specific circumstances he attributed to the sons of Zebedee (cf. Mk 3:17) and never used again, he never gave any of his disciples a new name.

Yet, he gave one to Simon, calling him "Cephas". This name was later translated into Greek as *Petros* and into Latin as *Petrus*. And it was translated precisely because it was not only a name; it was a "mandate" that *Petrus* received in that way from the Lord. The new name *Petrus* was to recur frequently in the Gospels and ended by replacing "Simon", his original name.

This fact acquires special importance if one bears in mind that in the Old Testament, a change of name usually preceded the entrustment of a mission (cf. Gn 17:5; 32:28ff., etc.).

Indeed, many signs indicate Christ's desire to give Peter special prominence within the Apostolic College: in Capernaum the Teacher enters Peter's house (cf. Mk 1:29); when the crowd presses around him on the shore of Lake Gennesaret, seeing two boats moored there, Jesus chooses Simon's (cf. Lk 5:3); when, on certain occasions, Jesus takes only three disciples with him, Peter is always recorded as the first of the group: as in the raising of Jairus' daughter (cf. Mk 5:37; Lk 8:51), in the Transfiguration (cf. Mk 9:2; Mt 17:1; Lk 9:28), and during the agony in the Garden of Gethsemane (cf. Mk 14:33; Mt 26:37). And again: the Temple tax collectors address Peter, and the Teacher pays only for himself and Peter (cf. Mt 17:24–27); it is Peter's feet that he washes first at the Last Supper (cf. Jn 13:6), and for Peter alone he prays that his faith will not fail so that he will be able to strengthen the other disciples in faith (cf. Lk 22:30–31).

Moreover, Peter himself was aware of his special position: he often also spoke on behalf of the others, asking for the explanation of a difficult parable (cf. Mt 15:15), the exact meaning of a precept (cf. Mt 18:21), or the formal promise of a reward (cf. Mt 19:27).

It is Peter in particular who resolves certain embarrassing situations by intervening on behalf of all. Thus, when Jesus, saddened by the misunderstanding of the crowd after the Bread of Life discourse, asks: "Will you also go away?" Peter's answer is peremptory in tone: "Lord, to whom shall we go? You have the words of eternal life" (cf. Jn 6:67–69).

Equally decisive is the profession of faith which, again on behalf of the Twelve, he makes near Caesarea Philippi. To Jesus' question: "But who do you say that I am?" Peter answers: "You are the Christ, the Son of the living God" (Mt 16:15–16). Jesus responded by pronouncing the solemn declaration that defines Peter's role in the Church once and for all: "And I tell you: you are Peter, and on this rock I will build my Church. . . . I will give you the keys of the Kingdom of Heaven, and whatever you bind on earth will be bound in heaven, and whatever you loose on earth will be loosed in heaven" (Mt 16:18–19).

In themselves, the three metaphors that Jesus uses are crystal clear: Peter will be the *rocky foundation* on which he will build the edifice of the Church; he will have *the keys* of the Kingdom of Heaven to open or close it to people as he sees fit; lastly, he will be able to *bind* or to *loose*, in the sense of establishing or prohibiting whatever he deems necessary for the life of the Church. It is always Christ's Church, not Peter's.

Thus, vivid images portray what the subsequent reflection will describe by the term: "primacy of jurisdiction".

This pre-eminent position that Jesus wanted to bestow upon Peter is also encountered after the Resurrection: Jesus charges the women to announce it especially to Peter, as distinct from the other Apostles (cf. Mk 16:7); it is to Peter and John that Mary Magdalene runs to tell them that the stone has been rolled away from the entrance to the tomb (cf. Jn 20:2), and John was to stand back to let Peter enter first when they arrived at the empty tomb (cf. Jn 20:4–6).

Then, Peter was to be the first witness of an appearance of the Risen One (cf. Lk 24:34; 1 Cor 15:5). His role, decisively emphasized (cf. Jn 20:3–10), marks the continuity between the pre-eminence he had in the group of the Apostles and the pre-eminence he would continue to have in the community born with the Paschal events, as the Book of Acts testifies (cf. 1:15–26; 2:14–40; 3:12–26; 4:8–12; 5:1–11, 29; 8:14–17; 10; etc.).

His behavior was considered so decisive that it prompted remarks as well as criticism (cf. Acts 11:1–18; Gal 2:11–14).

At the so-called Council of Jerusalem Peter played a directive role (cf. Acts 15; Gal 2:1–10), and precisely because he was a witness of authentic faith, Paul himself recognized that he had a certain quality of "leadership" (cf. 1 Cor 15:5; Gal 1:18; 2:7ff., etc.).

Moreover, the fact that several of the key texts that refer to Peter can be traced back to the context of the Last Supper, during which Christ conferred upon Peter the ministry of strengthening his brethren (cf. Lk 22:31ff.), shows that the ministry entrusted to Peter was one of the constitutive elements of the Church, which was born from the commemoration of the Pasch celebrated in the Eucharist.

This contextualization of the Primacy of Peter at the Last Supper, at the moment of the institution of the Eucharist, the Lord's Pasch, also points to the ultimate meaning of this Primacy: Peter must be the custodian of communion with Christ for all time. He must guide people to communion with Christ; he must ensure that the net does not break and, consequently, that universal communion endures. Only together can we be with Christ, who is Lord of all.

Thus, Peter is responsible for guaranteeing communion with Christ with the love of Christ, guiding people to fulfill this love in everyday life. Let us pray that the Primacy of Peter, entrusted to poor human beings, will always be exercised in this original sense as the Lord desired and that its true meaning will therefore always be recognized by the brethren who are not yet in full communion with us.

Andrew, the Protoclete

Dear Brothers and Sisters,

In the last two Catecheses we spoke about the figure of Saint Peter. Now, in the measure that sources allow us, we want to know the other eleven Apostles a bit better. Therefore, today we shall speak of Simon Peter's brother, Saint Andrew, who was also one of the Twelve.

The first striking characteristic of Andrew is his name: it is not Hebrew, as might have been expected, but Greek, indicative of a certain cultural openness in his family that cannot be ignored. We are in Galilee, where the Greek language and culture are quite present. Andrew comes second in the list of the Twelve, as in Matthew (10:1–4) and in Luke (6:13–16); or fourth, as in Mark (3:13–18) and in the Acts (1:13–14). In any case, he certainly enjoyed great prestige within the early Christian communities.

The kinship between Peter and Andrew, as well as the joint call that Jesus addressed to them, are explicitly mentioned in the Gospels. We read: "As he walked by the Sea of Galilee, he saw two brothers, Simon who is called Peter and Andrew his brother, casting a net into the sea; for they were fishermen. And he said to them, 'Follow me, and I will make you fishers of men'" (Mt 4:18–19; Mk 1:16–17).

From the Fourth Gospel we know another important detail: Andrew had previously been a disciple of John the

Baptist: and this shows us that he was a man who was searching, who shared in Israel's hope, who wanted to know better the word of the Lord, the presence of the Lord.

He was truly a man of faith and hope; and one day he heard John the Baptist proclaiming Jesus as: "the Lamb of God" (Jn 1:36); so he was stirred and, with another unnamed disciple, followed Jesus, the one whom John had called "the Lamb of God". The Evangelist says that "they saw where he was staying; and they stayed with him that day . . ." (Jn 1:37–39).

Thus, Andrew enjoyed precious moments of intimacy with Jesus. The account continues with one important annotation: "One of the two who heard John speak, and followed him, was Andrew, Simon Peter's brother. He first found his brother Simon, and said to him, 'We have found the Messiah' (which means Christ). He brought him to Jesus" (Jn 1:40–43), straightaway showing an unusual apostolic spirit.

Andrew, then, was the first of the Apostles to be called to follow Jesus. Exactly for this reason the liturgy of the Byzantine Church honors him with the nickname: *Protokletos* [*protoclete*], which means, precisely, "the first called".

And it is certain that it is partly because of the family tie between Peter and Andrew that the Church of Rome and the Church of Constantinople feel one another in a special way to be Sister Churches. To emphasize this relationship, my Predecessor Pope Paul VI, in 1964, returned the important relic of Saint Andrew, which until then had been kept in the Vatican Basilica, to the Orthodox Metropolitan Bishop of the city of Patras in Greece, where tradition has it that the Apostle was crucified.

The Gospel traditions mention Andrew's name in particular on another three occasions that tell us something more about this man. The first is that of the multiplication of the loaves in Galilee. On that occasion, it was Andrew who pointed out to Jesus the presence of a young boy who had with him five barley loaves and two fish: not much, he remarked, for the multitudes who had gathered in that place (cf. Jn 6:8–9).

In this case, it is worth highlighting Andrew's realism. He noticed the boy, that is, he had already asked the question: "but what good is that for so many?" (*ibid.*), and recognized the insufficiency of his minimal resources. Jesus, however, knew how to make them sufficient for the multitude of people who had come to hear him.

The second occasion was at Jerusalem. As he left the city, a disciple drew Jesus' attention to the sight of the massive walls that supported the Temple. The Teacher's response was surprising: he said that of those walls not one stone would be left upon another. Then Andrew, together with Peter, James, and John, questioned him: "Tell us, when will this be, and what will be the sign when these things are all to be accomplished?" (Mk 13:1–4).

In answer to this question Jesus gave an important discourse on the destruction of Jerusalem and on the end of the world, in which he asked his disciples to be wise in interpreting the signs of the times and to be constantly on their guard.

From this event we can deduce that we should not be afraid to ask Jesus questions but at the same time that we must be ready to accept even the surprising and difficult teachings that he offers us.

Lastly, a third initiative of Andrew is recorded in the Gospels: the scene is still Jerusalem, shortly before the Passion. For the Feast of the Passover, John recounts, some Greeks had come to the city, probably proselytes or God-fearing men who had come up to worship the God of Israel at the Passover Feast. Andrew and Philip, the two Apostles with Greek names, served as interpreters and mediators of this small group of Greeks with Jesus.

The Lord's answer to their question—as so often in John's Gospel—appears enigmatic, but precisely in this way proves full of meaning. Jesus said to the two disciples and, through them, to the Greek world: "The hour has come for the Son of man to be glorified. I solemnly assure you, unless a grain of wheat falls to the earth and dies, it remains just a grain of wheat; but if it dies, it produces much fruit" (12:23–24).

Jesus wants to say: Yes, my meeting with the Greeks will take place, but not as a simple, brief conversation between myself and a few others, motivated above all by curiosity. The hour of my glorification will come with my death, which can be compared with the falling into the earth of a grain of wheat. My death on the Cross will bring forth great fruitfulness: in the Resurrection the "dead grain of wheat"—a symbol of myself crucified—will become the bread of life for the world; it will be a light for the peoples and cultures.

Yes, the encounter with the Greek soul, with the Greek world, will be achieved in that profundity to which the grain of wheat refers, which attracts to itself the forces of heaven and earth and becomes bread.

In other words, Jesus was prophesying about the Church of the Greeks, the Church of the pagans, the Church of the world, as a fruit of his Pasch.

Some very ancient traditions not only see Andrew, who communicated these words to the Greeks, as the interpreter of some Greeks at the meeting with Jesus recalled here, but consider him the Apostle to the Greeks in the years subsequent to Pentecost. They enable us to know that for the rest of his life he was the preacher and interpreter of Jesus for the Greek world.

Peter, his brother, traveled from Jerusalem through

Antioch and reached Rome to exercise his universal mission; Andrew, instead, was the Apostle of the Greek world. So it is that in life and in death they appear as true brothers—a brotherhood that is symbolically expressed in the special reciprocal relations of the Sees of Rome and of Constantinople, which are truly Sister Churches.

A later tradition, as has been mentioned, tells of Andrew's death at Patras, where he too suffered the torture of crucifixion. At that supreme moment, however, like his brother, Peter, he asked to be nailed to a cross different from the Cross of Jesus. In his case it was a diagonal or X-shaped cross, which has thus come to be known as "Saint Andrew's cross".

This is what the Apostle is claimed to have said on that occasion, according to an ancient story (which dates back to the beginning of the sixth century), entitled *The Passion of Andrew*:

> Hail, O Cross, inaugurated by the Body of Christ and adorned with his limbs as though they were precious pearls. Before the Lord mounted you, you inspired an earthly fear. Now, instead, endowed with heavenly love, you are accepted as a gift.
>
> Believers know of the great joy that you possess, and of the multitude of gifts you have prepared. I come to you, therefore, confident and joyful, so that you too may receive me exultant as a disciple of the One who was hung upon you. . . . O blessed Cross, clothed in the majesty and beauty of the Lord's limbs! . . . Take me, carry me far from men, and restore me to my Teacher, so that, through you, the one who redeemed me by you, may receive me. Hail, O Cross; yes, hail indeed!

Here, as can be seen, is a very profound Christian spirituality. It does not view the Cross as an instrument of torture but rather as the incomparable means for perfect configuration to the Redeemer, to the grain of wheat that fell into the earth.

Here we have a very important lesson to learn: our own crosses acquire value if we consider them and accept them as a part of the Cross of Christ, if a reflection of his light illuminates them.

It is by that Cross alone that our sufferings too are ennobled and acquire their true meaning.

The Apostle Andrew, therefore, teaches us to follow Jesus with promptness (cf. Mt 4:20; Mk 1:18), to speak enthusiastically about him to those we meet, and especially, to cultivate a relationship of true familiarity with him, acutely aware that in him alone can we find the ultimate meaning of our life and death.

James, the Greater

WEDNESDAY, 21 JUNE 2006

Dear Brothers and Sisters,

We are continuing the series of portraits of the Apostles chosen directly by Jesus during his earthly life. We have spoken of Saint Peter and of his brother, Andrew. Today we meet the figure of James. The biblical lists of the Twelve mention two people with this name: James, son of Zebedee, and James, son of Alphaeus (cf. Mk 3:17, 18; Mt 10:2–3), who are commonly distinguished with the nicknames "James the Greater" and "James the Lesser".

These titles are certainly not intended to measure their holiness, but simply to state the different importance they receive in the writings of the New Testament and, in particular, in the setting of Jesus' earthly life. Today we will focus our attention on the first of these two figures with the same name.

The name "James" is the translation of *Iakobos*, the Grecised form of the name of the famous Patriarch Jacob. The Apostle of this name was the brother of John and, in the above-mentioned lists, comes second, immediately after Peter, as occurs in Mark (3:17); or in the third place, after Peter and Andrew, as in the Gospels of Matthew (10:2) and Luke (6:14), while in the Acts he comes after Peter and John (1:13). This James belongs, together with Peter and John, to the group of the three privileged disciples whom Jesus admitted to important moments in his life.

Since it is very hot today, I want to be brief and to mention here only two of these occasions. James was able to take part, together with Peter and John, in Jesus' Agony in the Garden of Gethsemane and in the event of Jesus' Transfiguration. Thus, it is a question of situations very different from each other: in one case, James, together with the other two Apostles, experiences the Lord's glory and sees him talking to Moses and Elijah; he sees the divine splendor shining out in Jesus.

On the other occasion, he finds himself face to face with suffering and humiliation; he sees with his own eyes how the Son of God humbles himself, making himself obedient unto death. The latter experience was certainly an opportunity for him to grow in faith, to adjust the unilateral, triumphalist interpretation of the former experience: he had to discern that the Messiah, whom the Jewish people were awaiting as a victor, was in fact surrounded not only by honor and glory, but also by suffering and weakness. Christ's glory was fulfilled precisely on the Cross, in his sharing in our sufferings.

This growth in faith was brought to completion by the Holy Spirit at Pentecost, so that James, when the moment of supreme witness came, would not draw back. Early in the first century, in the 40s, King Herod Agrippa, the grandson of Herod the Great, as Luke tells us, "laid violent hands upon some who belonged to the Church. He had James, the brother of John, killed by the sword" (Acts 12:1–2).

The brevity of the news, devoid of any narrative detail, reveals, on the one hand, how normal it was for Christians to witness to the Lord with their own lives and, on the other, that James had a position of relevance in the Church of Jerusalem, partly because of the role he played during Jesus' earthly existence.

A later tradition, dating back at least to Isidore of Seville, speaks of a visit he made to Spain to evangelize that important region of the Roman Empire. According to another tradition, it was his body instead that had been taken to Spain, to the city of Santiago de Compostela.

As we all know, that place became the object of great veneration and is still the destination of numerous pilgrimages, not only from Europe but from the whole world. This explains the iconographical representation of Saint James with the pilgrim's staff and the scroll of the Gospel in hand, typical features of the traveling Apostle dedicated to the proclamation of the "Good News" and characteristics of the pilgrimage of Christian life.

Consequently, we can learn much from Saint James: promptness in accepting the Lord's call even when he asks us to leave the "boat" of our human securities, enthusiasm in following him on the paths that he indicates to us over and above any deceptive presumption of our own, readiness to witness to him with courage, if necessary to the point of making the supreme sacrifice of life.

Thus James the Greater stands before us as an eloquent example of generous adherence to Christ. He, who initially had requested, through his mother, to be seated with his brother next to the Master in his Kingdom, was precisely the first to drink the chalice of the Passion and to share martyrdom with the Apostles.

And, in the end, summarizing everything, we can say that the journey, not only exterior but above all interior, from the mount of the Transfiguration to the mount of the Agony, symbolizes the entire pilgrimage of Christian life, among the persecutions of the world and the consolations of God, as the Second Vatican Council says. In following Jesus, like Saint James, we know that even in difficulties we are on the right path.

13

James, the Lesser

WEDNESDAY, 28 JUNE 2006

Dear Brothers and Sisters,

Beside the figure of James the Greater, son of Zebedee, of whom we spoke last Wednesday, another James appears in the Gospels, known as "the Lesser". He is also included in the list of the Twelve Apostles personally chosen by Jesus and is always specified as "the son of Alphaeus" (Mt 10:3; Mk 3:18; Lk 5; Acts 1:13). He has often been identified with another James, called "the Younger" (cf. Mk 15:40), the son of a Mary (cf. *ibid.*), possibly "Mary the wife of Clopas", who stood, according to the Fourth Gospel, at the foot of the Cross with the Mother of Jesus (cf. Jn 19:25).

He also came from Nazareth and was probably related to Jesus (cf. Mt 13:55; Mk 6:3); according to Semitic custom he is called "brother" (Mk 6:3; Gal 1:19).

The book of the Acts of the Apostles emphasizes the prominent role that this latter James played in the Church of Jerusalem. At the Apostolic Council celebrated there after the death of James the Greater he declared, together with the others, that pagans could be received into the Church without first submitting to circumcision (cf. Acts 15:13). Saint Paul, who attributes a specific appearance of the Risen One to James (cf. 1 Cor 15:7), even named James before Cephas-Peter on the occasion of his visit to Jerusalem, describing him as a "pillar" of that Church on a par with Peter (cf. Gal 2:9).

Subsequently, Judeo-Christians considered him their main reference point. The Letter that bears the name of James is also attributed to him and is included in the New Testament canon. In it, he is not presented as a "brother of the Lord" but as a "servant of God and of the Lord Jesus Christ" (Jas 1:1).

Among experts, the question of the identity of these two figures with the same name, James son of Alphaeus and James "the brother of the Lord", is disputed. With reference to the period of Jesus' earthly life, the Gospel traditions have not kept for us any account of either one of them.

The Acts of the Apostles, on the other hand, reveal that a "James" played a very important role in the early Church, as we have already mentioned, after the Resurrection of Jesus (cf. Acts 12:17; 15:13–21; 21:18).

His most important act was his intervention in the matter of the difficult relations between the Christians of Jewish origin and those of pagan origin: in this matter, together with Peter, he contributed to overcoming, or rather, to integrating the original Jewish dimension of Christianity with the need not to impose upon converted pagans the obligation to submit to all the norms of the Law of Moses. The Book of Acts has preserved for us the solution of compromise proposed precisely by James and accepted by all the Apostles present, according to which pagans who believed in Jesus Christ were to be asked only to abstain from the idolatrous practice of eating the meat of animals offered in sacrifice to the gods, and from "impropriety", a term which probably alluded to irregular matrimonial unions. In practice, it was a question of adhering to only a few prohibitions of Mosaic Law held to be very important.

Thus, two important and complementary results were obtained, both of which are still valid today: on the one hand, the inseparable relationship that binds Christianity to the Jewish religion, as to a perennially alive and effective matrix, was recognized; and on the other, Christians of pagan origin were permitted to keep their own sociological identity which they would have lost had they been forced to observe the so-called "ceremonial precepts" of Moses.

Henceforth, these precepts were no longer to be considered binding for converted pagans. In essence, this gave rise to a practice of reciprocal esteem and respect which, despite subsequent regrettable misunderstandings, aimed by its nature to safeguard what was characteristic of each one of the two parties.

The oldest information on the death of this James is given to us by the Jewish historian Flavius Josephus. In his *Jewish Antiquities* (20, 201ff.), written in Rome towards the end of the first century, he says that the death of James was decided with an illegal initiative by the High Priest Ananus, a son of the Ananias attested to in the Gospels; in the year 62, he profited from the gap between the deposition of one Roman Procurator (Festus) and the arrival of his successor (Albinus) to hand him over for stoning.

As well as the apocryphal Proto-Gospel of James, which exalts the holiness and virginity of Mary, Mother of Jesus, the Letter that bears his name is particularly associated with the name of this James. In the canon of the New Testament, it occupies the first place among the so-called "Catholic Letters", that is, those that were not addressed to any single particular Church—such as Rome, Ephesus, etc.—but to many Churches.

It is quite an important writing which heavily insists on the need not to reduce our faith to a purely verbal or abstract declaration, but to express it in practice in good works. Among other things, he invites us to be constant in trials, joyfully accepted, and to pray with trust to obtain from God the gift of wisdom, thanks to which we succeed in understanding that the true values of life are not to be found in transient riches but rather in the ability to share our possessions with the poor and the needy (cf. Jas 1:27).

Thus, Saint James' Letter shows us a very concrete and practical Christianity. Faith must be fulfilled in life, above all, in love of neighbor and especially in dedication to the poor. It is against this background that the famous sentence must be read: "As the body apart from the spirit is dead, so faith apart from works is dead" (Jas 2:26).

At times, this declaration by Saint James has been considered as opposed to the affirmations of Paul, who claims that we are justified by God not by virtue of our actions but through our faith (cf. Gal 2:16; Rom 3:28). However, if the two apparently contradictory sentences with their different perspectives are correctly interpreted, they actually complete each other.

Saint Paul is opposed to the pride of man who thinks he does not need the love of God that precedes us; he is opposed to the pride of self-justification without grace, simply given and undeserved.

Saint James, instead, talks about works as the normal fruit of faith: "Every sound tree bears good fruit, but the bad tree bears evil fruit", the Lord says (Mt 7:17). And Saint James repeats it and says it to us.

Lastly, the Letter of James urges us to abandon ourselves in the hands of God in all that we do: "If the Lord wills" (Jas 4:15). Thus, he teaches us not to presume to plan our lives autonomously and with self interest, but to make room for the inscrutable will of God, who knows what is truly good for us.

In this way, Saint James remains an ever up-to-date teacher of life for each one of us.

14

John, Son of Zebedee

WEDNESDAY, 5 JULY 2006

Dear Brothers and Sisters,

Let us dedicate our meeting today to remembering another very important member of the Apostolic College: John, son of Zebedee and brother of James. His typically Jewish name means: "the Lord has worked grace". He was mending his nets on the shore of Lake Tiberias when Jesus called him and his brother (cf. Mt 4:21; Mk 1:19).

John was always among the small group that Jesus took with him on specific occasions. He was with Peter and James when Jesus entered Peter's house in Capernaum to cure his mother-in-law (cf. Mk 1:29); with the other two, he followed the Teacher into the house of Jairus, a ruler of the synagogue whose daughter he was to bring back to life (cf. Mk 5:37); he followed him when he climbed the mountain for his Transfiguration (cf. Mk 9:2).

He was beside the Lord on the Mount of Olives when, before the impressive sight of the Temple of Jerusalem, he spoke of the end of the city and of the world (cf. Mk 13:3); and, lastly, he was close to him in the Garden of Gethsemane when he withdrew to pray to the Father before the Passion (cf. Mk 14:33).

Shortly before the Passover, when Jesus chose two disciples to send them to prepare the room for the Supper, it was to him and to Peter that he entrusted this task (cf. Lk 22:8).

His prominent position in the group of the Twelve makes it somewhat easier to understand the initiative taken one day by his mother: she approached Jesus to ask him if her two sons—John and James—could sit next to him in the Kingdom, one on his right and one on his left (cf. Mt 20:20–21).

As we know, Jesus answered by asking a question in turn: he asked whether they were prepared to drink the cup that he was about to drink (cf. Mt 20:22). The intention behind those words was to open the two disciples' eyes, to introduce them to knowledge of the mystery of his person and to suggest their future calling to be his witnesses, even to the supreme trial of blood.

A little later, in fact, Jesus explained that he had not come to be served, but to serve and to give his life as a ransom for many (cf. Mt 20:28).

In the days after the Resurrection, we find "the sons of Zebedee" busy with Peter and some of the other disciples on a night when they caught nothing, but that was followed, after the intervention of the Risen One, by the miraculous catch: it was to be "the disciple Jesus loved" who first recognized "the Lord" and pointed him out to Peter (cf. Jn 21:1–13).

In the Church of Jerusalem, John occupied an important position in supervising the first group of Christians. Indeed, Paul lists him among those whom he calls the "pillars" of that community (cf. Gal 2:9). In fact, Luke in the Acts presents him together with Peter while they are going to pray in the Temple (cf. Acts 3:1–4, 11) or appear before the Sanhedrin to witness to their faith in Jesus Christ (cf. Acts 4:13, 19).

Together with Peter, he is sent to the Church of Jerusalem to strengthen the people in Samaria who had accepted the Gospel, praying for them that they might receive the Holy Spirit (cf. Acts 8:14–15). In particular, we should remember what he affirmed with Peter to the Sanhedrin members who were accusing them: "We cannot but speak of what we have seen and heard" (Acts 4:20).

It is precisely this frankness in confessing his faith that lives on as an example and a warning for all of us always to be ready to declare firmly our steadfast attachment to Christ, putting faith before any human calculation or concern.

According to tradition, John is the "disciple whom Jesus loved", who in the Fourth Gospel laid his head against the Teacher's breast at the Last Supper (cf. Jn 13:23), stood at the foot of the Cross together with the Mother of Jesus (cf. Jn 19:25), and lastly, witnessed both the empty tomb and the presence of the Risen One himself (cf. Jn 20:2; 21:7).

We know that this identification is disputed by scholars today, some of whom view him merely as the prototype of a disciple of Jesus. Leaving the exegetes to settle the matter, let us be content here with learning an important lesson for our lives: the Lord wishes to make each one of us a disciple who lives in personal friendship with him.

To achieve this, it is not enough to follow him and to listen to him outwardly: it is also necessary to live with him and like him. This is only possible in the context of a relationship of deep familiarity, imbued with the warmth of total trust. This is what happens between friends; for this reason Jesus said one day: "Greater love has no man than this, that a man lay down his life for his friends. . . . No longer do I call you servants, for the servant does not know what his master is doing; but I have called you friends, for all that I have heard from my Father I have made known to you" (Jn 15:13, 15).

In the apocryphal *Acts of John*, the Apostle is not presented as the founder of Churches or as the guide of already established communities, but as a perpetual wayfarer, a communicator of the faith in the encounter with "souls capable of hoping and of being saved" (18:10; 23:8).

All is motivated by the paradoxical intention to make visible the invisible. And indeed, the Oriental Church calls him quite simply "the Theologian", that is, the one who can speak in accessible terms of the divine, revealing an arcane access to God through attachment to Jesus.

Devotion to the Apostle John spread from the city of Ephesus where, according to an ancient tradition, he worked for many years and died in the end at an extraordinarily advanced age, during the reign of the Emperor Trajan.

In Ephesus in the sixth century, the Emperor Justinian had a great basilica built in his honor, whose impressive ruins are still standing today. Precisely in the East, he enjoyed and still enjoys great veneration.

In Byzantine iconography he is often shown as very elderly—according to tradition, he died under the Emperor Trajan—in the process of intense contemplation, in the attitude, as it were, of those asking for silence.

Indeed, without sufficient recollection it is impossible to approach the supreme mystery of God and of his revelation. This explains why, years ago, Athenagoras, Ecumenical Patriarch of Constantinople, the man whom Pope Paul VI embraced at a memorable encounter, said: "John is the origin of our loftiest spirituality. Like him, 'the silent ones' experience that mysterious exchange of hearts, pray for John's presence, and their hearts are set on fire" (O. Clément, *Dialoghi con Atenagora*, Turin 1972, p. 159).

May the Lord help us to study at John's school and learn the great lesson of love, so as to feel we are loved by Christ "to the end" (Jn 13:1), and spend our lives for him.

15

John, the Theologian

WEDNESDAY, 9 AUGUST 2006
Paul VI Audience Hall

Dear Brothers and Sisters,

Before the holidays I had begun sketching small portraits of the Twelve Apostles. The Apostles were Jesus' traveling companions, Jesus' friends. Their journey with Jesus was not only a physical journey from Galilee to Jerusalem, but an interior journey during which they learned faith in Jesus Christ, not without difficulty, for they were people like us.

But for this very reason, because they were Jesus' traveling companions, Jesus' friends, who learned faith on a journey that was far from easy, they are also guides for us, who help us to know Jesus Christ, to love him, and to have faith in him.

I have already commented on four of the Twelve Apostles: Simon Peter; Andrew, his brother; James, the brother of Saint John; and the other James, known as "The Lesser", who wrote a Letter that we find in the New Testament. And I had started to speak about John the Evangelist, gathering together in the last Catechesis before the holidays the essential facts for this Apostle's profile.

I would now like to focus attention on the content of his teaching. The writings that we want to examine today, therefore, are the Gospel and the Letters that go under his name.

If there is one characteristic topic that emerges from John's writings, it is love. It is not by chance that I wanted to begin my first Encyclical Letter with this Apostle's words, "God is love (*Deus caritas est*); he who abides in love abides in God, and God abides in him" (1 Jn 4:16). It is very difficult to find texts of this kind in other religions. Thus, words such as these bring us face to face with an element that is truly peculiar to Christianity.

John, of course, is not the only author of Christian origin to speak of love. Since this is an essential constituent of Christianity, all the New Testament writers speak of it, although with different emphases.

If we are now pausing to reflect on this subject in John, it is because he has outlined its principal features insistently and incisively. We therefore trust his words. One thing is certain: he does not provide an abstract, philosophical, or even theological treatment of what love is.

No, he is not a theoretician. True love, in fact, by its nature is never purely speculative but makes a direct, concrete, and even verifiable reference to real persons. Well, John, as an Apostle and a friend of Jesus, makes us see what its components are, or rather, the phases of Christian love, a movement marked by three moments.

The first concerns the very Source of love which the Apostle identifies as God, arriving at the affirmation that "God is love" (1 Jn 4:8, 16). John is the only New Testament author who gives us definitions of God. He says, for example, that "God is spirit" (Jn 4:24) or that "God is light" (1 Jn 1:5). Here he proclaims with radiant insight that "God is love."

Take note: it is not merely asserted that "God loves", or even less that "love is God"! In other words: John does not limit himself to describing the divine action but goes to its roots.

Moreover, he does not intend to attribute a divine quality

to a generic and even impersonal love; he does not rise from love to God, but turns directly to God to define his nature with the infinite dimension of love.

By so doing, John wants to say that the essential constituent of God is love and, hence, that all God's activity is born from love and impressed with love: all that God does, he does out of love and with love, even if we are not always immediately able to understand that this is love, true love.

At this point, however, it is indispensable to take another step and explain that God has concretely demonstrated his love by entering human history through the Person of Jesus Christ, incarnate, dead, and risen for us.

This is the second constitutive moment of God's love. He did not limit himself to verbal declarations but, we can say, truly committed himself and "paid" in the first person.

Exactly as John writes, "God so loved the world", that is, all of us, "that he gave his only Son" (Jn 3:16). Henceforth, God's love for humanity is concretized and manifested in the love of Jesus himself.

Again, John writes: "Having loved his own who were in the world, he loved them to the end" (Jn 13:1). By virtue of this oblative and total love we are radically ransomed from sin, as Saint John writes further: "My little children . . . if any one does sin, we have an advocate with the Father, Jesus Christ, the righteous; and he is the expiation for our sins, and not for ours only but also for the sins of the whole world" (1 Jn 2:1–2; cf. 1 Jn 1:7).

This is how Jesus' love for us reaches us: by the pouring out of his own Blood for our salvation! The Christian, pausing in contemplation before this "excess" of love, cannot but wonder what the proper response is. And I think each one of us, always and over and over again, must ask himself this.

This question introduces us into the third moment of the dynamic of love: from being the recipients of a love that precedes and surpasses us, we are called to the commitment of an active response which, to be adequate, can only be a response of love.

John speaks of a "commandment". He is, in fact, referring to these words of Jesus: "A new commandment I give to you, that you love one another; even as I have loved you, that you also love one another" (Jn 13:34).

Where is the newness to which Jesus refers? It lies in the fact that he is not content with repeating what had already been requested in the Old Testament and which we also read in the other Gospels: "You shall love your neighbor as yourself" (Lv 19:18; cf. Mt 22:37–39; Mk 12:29–31; Lk 10:27).

In the ancient precept the standard criterion was based on man ("as yourself"), whereas in the precept to which John refers, Jesus presents his own Person as the reason for and norm of our love: "as I have loved you".

It is in this way that love becomes truly Christian: both in the sense that it must be directed to all without distinction, and above all since it must be carried through to its extreme consequences, having no other bounds than being boundless.

Those words of Jesus, "as I have loved you", simultaneously invite and disturb us; they are a Christological goal that can appear unattainable, but at the same time they are an incentive that does not allow us to ensconce ourselves in what we have been able to achieve. It does not permit us to be content with what we are but spurs us to keep advancing towards this goal.

In *The Imitation of Christ*, that golden text of spirituality which is the small book dating back to the late Middle Ages, on this subject is written: "The love of Jesus is noble and generous: it spurs us on to do great things, and excites us to desire always that which is most perfect. Love will tend upwards and is not to be detained by things beneath. Love will be at liberty and free from all worldly affections . . . for love proceeds from God and cannot rest but in God above all things created. The lover flies, runs and rejoices, he is free and not held. He gives all for all and has all in all, because he rests in one sovereign good above all, from whom all good flows and proceeds" (Thomas à Kempis, *The Imitation of Christ*, Book III, Chapter V, 3–4).

What better comment could there be on the "new commandment" spelled out by John? Let us pray to the Father to be able, even if always imperfectly, to live it so intensely that we share it with those we meet on our way.

16

John, the Seer of Patmos

WEDNESDAY, 23 AUGUST 2006

Paul VI Audience Hall

Dear Brothers and Sisters,

In the last Catechesis we had reached the meditation on the figure of the Apostle John. We had first sought to look at all that can be known of his life. Then, in a second Catechesis, we meditated on the central content of his Gospel and his Letters: charity, love. And today we are still concerned with the figure of John, this time to examine the Seer of the Book of Revelation. And let us immediately note that while neither the Fourth Gospel nor the Letters attributed to the Apostle ever bear his name, the Book of Revelation makes at least four references to it (cf. 1:1, 4, 9; 22:8).

It is obvious, on the one hand, that the author had no reason not to mention his own name and, on the other, that he knew his first readers would be able precisely to identify him. We know, moreover, that in the third century, scholars were already disputing the true factual identity of John of the "Apocalypse".

For the sake of convenience we could also call him "the Seer of Patmos" because he is linked to the name of this island in the Aegean See where, according to his own autobiographical account, he was, as it were, deported "on account of the word of God and the testimony of Jesus" (Rv 1:9).

It was on Patmos itself, "on the Lord's Day . . . caught up in ecstasy" (Rv 1:10), that John had a grandiose vision and heard extraordinary messages that were to have a strong influence on the history of the Church and of entire Western culture.

For example, from the title of his book—*Apocalypse, Revelation*—the words "apocalypse, apocalyptic" were introduced into our language and, although inaccurately, they call to mind the idea of an incumbent catastrophe.

The Book should be understood against the backdrop of the dramatic experiences of the seven Churches of Asia (Ephesus, Smyrna, Pergamum, Thyatira, Sardis, Philadelphia, Laodicea) which had to face serious difficulties at the end of the first century—persecutions and also inner tensions—in their witness to Christ.

John addresses them, showing acute pastoral sensitivity to the persecuted Christians, whom he exhorts to be steadfast in the faith and not to identify with the pagan world. His purpose is constituted once and for all by the revelation, starting with the death and Resurrection of Christ, of the meaning of human history.

The first and fundamental vision of John, in fact, concerns the figure of the Lamb who is slain yet standing (cf. Rv 5:6) and is placed before the throne on which God himself is already seated.

By saying this, John wants first of all to tell us two things: the first is that although Jesus was killed with an act of violence, instead of falling heavily to the ground, he paradoxically stands very firmly on his own feet because, with the Resurrection, he overcame death once and for all.

The other thing is that Jesus himself, precisely because he died and was raised, henceforth fully shares in the kingship and saving power of the Father. This is the fundamental vision.

On this earth, Jesus, the Son of God, is a defenseless, wounded, and dead Lamb. Yet he stands up straight, on his feet, before God's throne and shares in the divine power. He has the history of the world in his hands.

Thus, the Seer wants to tell us: Trust in Jesus, do not be afraid of the opposing powers, of persecution! The wounded and dead Lamb is victorious! Follow the Lamb Jesus, entrust yourselves to Jesus, take his path! Even if in this world he is only a Lamb who appears weak, it is he who triumphs!

The subject of one of the most important visions of the Book of Revelation is this Lamb in the act of opening a scroll, previously closed with seven seals that no one had been able to break open. John is even shown in tears, for he finds no one worthy of opening the scroll or reading it (cf. Rv 5:4).

History remains indecipherable, incomprehensible. No one can read it. Perhaps John's weeping before the mystery of a history so obscure expresses the Asian Churches' dismay at God's silence in the face of the persecutions to which they were exposed at that time.

It is a dismay that can clearly mirror our consternation in the face of the serious difficulties, misunderstandings, and hostility that the Church also suffers today in various parts of the world.

These are trials that the Church does not of course deserve, just as Jesus himself did not deserve his torture. However, they reveal both the wickedness of man, when he abandons himself to the promptings of evil, and also the superior ordering of events on God's part.

Well then, only the sacrificed Lamb can open the sealed scroll and reveal its content, give meaning to this history that so often seems senseless. He alone can draw from it instructions and teachings for the life of Christians, to whom his

victory over death brings the message and guarantee of
victory that they too will undoubtedly obtain. The whole of
the vividly imaginative language that John uses aims to offer
this consolation.

Also at the heart of the visions that the Book of Revelation
unfolds are the deeply significant vision of the Woman
bringing forth a male child and the complementary one of
the dragon, already thrown down from Heaven but still very
powerful.

This Woman represents Mary, the Mother of the Redeemer, but at the same time she also represents the whole
Church, the People of God of all times, the Church which in
all ages, with great suffering, brings forth Christ ever anew.
And she is always threatened by the dragon's power. She
appears defenseless and weak.

But while she is threatened, persecuted by the dragon, she
is also protected by God's comfort. And in the end this
Woman wins. The dragon does not win.

This is the great prophecy of this Book that inspires
confidence in us! The Woman who suffers in history, the
Church which is persecuted, appears in the end as the radiant
Bride, the figure of the new Jerusalem where there will be no
more mourning or weeping, an image of the world transformed, of the new world whose light is God himself, whose
lamp is the Lamb.

For this reason, although John's Book of Revelation is
pervaded by continuous references to suffering, tribulation,
and tears—the dark face of history—it is likewise permeated
by frequent songs of praise that symbolize, as it were, the
luminous face of history.

So it is, for example, that we read in it of a great multitude
that is singing, almost shouting: "Alleluia! For the Lord our
God the Almighty reigns. Let us rejoice and exult and give

him the glory, for the marriage of the Lamb has come, and his Bride has made herself ready" (Rv 19:6–7).

Here we face the typical Christian paradox, according to which suffering is never seen as the last word but, rather, as a transition towards happiness; indeed, suffering itself is already mysteriously mingled with the joy that flows from hope.

For this very reason John, the Seer of Patmos, can close his Book with a final aspiration, trembling with fearful expectation. He invokes the definitive coming of the Lord: "Come, Lord Jesus!" (Rv 22:20).

This was one of the central prayers of the nascent Christianity, also translated by Saint Paul into its Aramaic form: "*Marana tha*". And this prayer, "Our Lord, come!" (1 Cor 16:22), has many dimensions.

It is, naturally, first and foremost an expectation of the definitive victory of the Lord, of the new Jerusalem, of the Lord who comes and transforms the world. But at the same time, it is also a Eucharistic prayer: "Come Jesus, now!" And Jesus comes; he anticipates his definitive coming.

So it is that we say joyfully at the same time: "Come now and come for ever!"

This prayer also has a third meaning: "You have already come, Lord! We are sure of your presence among us. It is our joyous experience. But come definitively!"

And thus, let us too pray with Saint Paul, with the Seer of Patmos, with the newborn Christianity: "Come, Jesus! Come and transform the world! Come today already and may peace triumph!" Amen!

17

Matthew

Dear Brothers and Sisters,

Continuing the series of portraits of the Twelve Apostles that
we began a few weeks ago, let us reflect today on Matthew.
To tell the truth, it is almost impossible to paint a complete
picture of him because the information we have of him is
scarce and fragmentary. What we can do, however, is to
outline not so much his biography as, rather, the profile of
him that the Gospel conveys.

In the meantime, he always appears in the lists of the
Twelve chosen by Jesus (cf. Mt 10:3; Mk 3:18; Lk 6:15; Acts
1:13).

His name in Hebrew means "gift of God". The first
canonical Gospel, which goes under his name, presents him
to us in the list of the Twelve, labeled very precisely: "the tax
collector" (Mt 10:3).

Thus, Matthew is identified with the man sitting at the tax
office whom Jesus calls to follow him: "As Jesus passed on
from there, he saw a man called Matthew sitting at the tax
office; and he said to him, 'Follow me.' And he rose and
followed him" (Mt 9:9). Mark (cf. 2:13–17) and Luke (cf.
5:27–30) also tell of the calling of the man sitting at the tax
office, but they call him "Levi".

To imagine the scene described in Matthew 9:9, it suffices

to recall Caravaggio's magnificent canvas, kept here in Rome at the Church of Saint Louis of the French.

A further biographical detail emerges from the Gospels: in the passage that immediately precedes the account of the call, a miracle that Jesus worked at Capernaum is mentioned (cf. Mt 9:1–8; Mk 2:1–12) and the proximity to the Sea of Galilee, that is, the Lake of Tiberias (cf. Mk 2:13–14).

It is possible to deduce from this that Matthew exercised the function of tax collector at Capernaum, which was exactly located "by the sea" (Mt 4:13), where Jesus was a permanent guest at Peter's house.

On the basis of these simple observations that result from the Gospel, we can advance a pair of thoughts.

The first is that Jesus welcomes into the group of his close friends a man who, according to the concepts in vogue in Israel at that time, was regarded as a public sinner.

Matthew, in fact, not only handled money deemed impure because of its provenance from people foreign to the People of God, but he also collaborated with an alien and despicably greedy authority whose tributes, moreover, could be arbitrarily determined.

This is why the Gospels several times link "tax collectors and sinners" (Mt 9:10; Lk 15:1), as well as "tax collectors and prostitutes" (Mt 21:31).

Furthermore, they see publicans as an example of miserliness (cf. Mt 5:46: they only like those who like them) and mention one of them, Zacchaeus, as "a chief tax collector, and rich" (Lk 19:2), whereas popular opinion associated them with "extortioners, the unjust, adulterers" (Lk 18:11).

A first fact strikes one based on these references: Jesus does not exclude anyone from his friendship. Indeed, precisely while he is at table in the home of Matthew-Levi, in response to those who expressed shock at the fact that he associated with people who had so little to recommend them, he made the important statement: "Those who are well have no need of a physician, but those who are sick; I came not to call the righteous, but sinners" (Mk 2:17).

The good news of the Gospel consists precisely in this: offering God's grace to the sinner!

Elsewhere, with the famous words of the Pharisee and the publican who went up to the Temple to pray, Jesus actually indicates an anonymous tax collector as an appreciated example of humble trust in divine mercy: while the Pharisee is boasting of his own moral perfection, the "tax collector . . . would not even lift up his eyes to heaven, but beat his breast, saying, 'God, be merciful to me a sinner!'"

And Jesus comments: "I tell you, this man went down to his house justified rather than the other; for every one who exalts himself will be humbled, but he who humbles himself will be exalted" (Lk 18:13–14).

Thus, in the figure of Matthew, the Gospels present to us a true and proper paradox: those who seem to be the farthest from holiness can even become a model of the acceptance of God's mercy and offer a glimpse of its marvelous effects in their own lives.

Saint John Chrysostom makes an important point in this regard: he notes that only in the account of certain calls is the work of those concerned mentioned. Peter, Andrew, James, and John are called while they are fishing, while Matthew, while he is collecting tithes.

These are unimportant jobs, Chrysostom comments, "because there is nothing more despicable than the tax collector, and nothing more common than fishing" (*In Matth. Hom.*: *PL* 57, 363). Jesus' call, therefore, also reaches people of a low social class while they go about their ordinary work.

Another reflection prompted by the Gospel narrative is

that Matthew responds instantly to Jesus' call: "he rose and followed him." The brevity of the sentence clearly highlights Matthew's readiness in responding to the call. For him it meant leaving everything, especially what guaranteed him a reliable source of income, even if it was often unfair and dishonorable. Evidently, Matthew understood that familiarity with Jesus did not permit him to pursue activities of which God disapproved.

The application to the present day is easy to see: it is not permissible today either to be attached to things that are incompatible with the following of Jesus, as is the case with riches dishonestly achieved.

Jesus once said, mincing no words: "If you would be perfect, go, sell what you possess and give to the poor, and you will have treasure in heaven; and come, follow me" (Mt 19:21).

This is exactly what Matthew did: he rose and followed him! In this "he rose", it is legitimate to read detachment from a sinful situation and, at the same time, a conscious attachment to a new, upright life in communion with Jesus.

Lastly, let us remember that the tradition of the ancient Church agrees in attributing to Matthew the paternity of the First Gospel. This had already begun with Bishop Papias of Hierapolis in Frisia, in about the year 130.

He writes: "Matthew set down the words (of the Lord) in the Hebrew tongue and everyone interpreted them as best he could" (in Eusebius of Caesarea, *Hist. Eccl.*, III, 39, 16).

Eusebius, the historian, adds this piece of information: "When Matthew, who had first preached among the Jews, decided also to reach out to other peoples, he wrote down the Gospel he preached in his mother tongue; thus, he sought to put in writing, for those whom he was leaving, what they would be losing with his departure" (*ibid.*, III, 24, 6).

The Gospel of Matthew written in Hebrew or Aramaic is no longer extant, but in the Greek Gospel that we possess we still continue to hear, in a certain way, the persuasive voice of the publican Matthew, who, having become an Apostle, continues to proclaim God's saving mercy to us. And let us listen to Saint Matthew's message, meditating upon it ever anew also to learn to stand up and follow Jesus with determination.

18

Philip, the Apostle

WEDNESDAY, 6 SEPTEMBER 2006

Saint Peter's Square

Dear Brothers and Sisters,

While we continue to outline the features of the various Apostles, as we have been doing for several weeks, today we meet Philip. He always comes fifth in the lists of the Twelve (cf. Mt 10:3; Mk 3:18; Lk 6:14; Acts 1:13); hence, he is definitely among the first.

Although Philip was of Jewish origin, his name is Greek, like that of Andrew, and this is a small sign of cultural openness that must not be underestimated. The information we have on him is provided by John's Gospel. Like Peter and Andrew, he is a native of Bethsaida (cf. Jn 1:44), a town that belonged to the Tetrarchy of a son of Herod the Great, who was also called Philip (cf. Lk 3:1).

The Fourth Gospel recounts that after being called by Jesus, Philip meets Nathanael and tells him: "We have found him of whom Moses in the law and also the prophets wrote, Jesus of Nazareth, the son of Joseph" (Jn 1:45). Philip does not give way to Nathanael's somewhat sceptical answer ("Can anything good come out of Nazareth?") and firmly retorts: "Come and see!" (Jn 1:46).

In his dry but clear response, Philip displays the characteristics of a true witness: he is not satisfied with presenting the proclamation theoretically, but directly challenges the person addressing him by suggesting he have a personal experience of what he has been told.

The same two verbs are used by Jesus when two disciples of John the Baptist approach him to ask him where he is staying. Jesus answers: "Come and see" (cf. Jn 1:38–39).

We can imagine that Philip is also addressing us with those two verbs that imply personal involvement. He is also saying to us what he said to Nathanael: "Come and see." The Apostle engages us to become closely acquainted with Jesus.

In fact, friendship, true knowledge of the other person, needs closeness and indeed, to a certain extent, lives on it. Moreover, it should not be forgotten that according to what Mark writes, Jesus chose the Twelve primarily "to be with him" (Mk 3:14); that is, to share in his life and learn directly from him not only the style of his behavior, but above all who he really was.

Indeed, only in this way, taking part in his life, could they get to know him and, subsequently, proclaim him.

Later, in Paul's Letter to the Ephesians, one would read that what is important is to "learn Christ" (4:20): therefore, not only and not so much to listen to his teachings and words as rather to know him in person, that is, his humanity and his divinity, his mystery and his beauty. In fact, he is not only a Teacher but a Friend, indeed, a Brother.

How will we be able to get to know him properly by being distant? Closeness, familiarity, and habit make us discover the true identity of Jesus Christ. The Apostle Philip reminds us precisely of this. And thus he invites us to "come" and "see", that is, to enter into contact by listening, responding, and communion of life with Jesus, day by day.

Then, on the occasion of the multiplication of the loaves, he received a request from Jesus as precise as it was surprising: that is, where could they buy bread to satisfy the hunger of all the people who were following him (cf. Jn 6:5). Then Philip very realistically answered: "Two hundred denarii would not buy enough bread for each of them to get a little" (Jn 6:7).

Here one can see the practicality and realism of the Apostle, who can judge the effective implications of a situation.

We then know how things went. We know that Jesus took the loaves and, after giving thanks, distributed them. Thus, he brought about the multiplication of the loaves.

It is interesting, however, that it was to Philip himself that Jesus turned for some preliminary help with solving the problem: this is an obvious sign that he belonged to the close group that surrounded Jesus.

On another occasion very important for future history, before the Passion some Greeks who had gone to Jerusalem for the Passover "came to Philip . . . and said to him, 'Sir, we wish to see Jesus.' Philip went and told Andrew; Andrew went with Philip and they told Jesus" (cf. Jn 12:20–22).

Once again, we have an indication of his special prestige within the Apostolic College. In this case, Philip acts above all as an intermediary between the request of some Greeks— he probably spoke Greek and could serve as an interpreter— and Jesus; even if he joined Andrew, the other Apostle with a Greek name, he was in any case the one whom the foreigners addressed.

This teaches us always to be ready to accept questions and requests, wherever they come from, and to direct them to the Lord, the only one who can fully satisfy them. Indeed, it is important to know that the prayers of those who approach us are not ultimately addressed to us, but to the Lord: it is to him that we must direct anyone in need. So it is that each one of us must be an open road towards him!

There is then another very particular occasion when Philip makes his entrance. During the Last Supper, after Jesus affirmed that to know him was also to know the Father (cf. Jn 14:7), Philip quite ingenuously asks him: "Lord, show us the Father, and we shall be satisfied" (Jn 14:8). Jesus answered with a gentle rebuke: "Have I been with you so long, and yet you do not know me, Philip? He who has seen me has seen the Father; how can you say, 'Show us the Father'? Do you not believe that I am in the Father and the Father in me? . . . Believe me that I am in the Father and the Father in me" (Jn 14:9–11).

These words are among the most exalted in John's Gospel. They contain a true and proper revelation. At the end of the Prologue to his Gospel, John says: "No one has ever seen God; the only Son, who is in the bosom of the Father, he has made him known" (Jn 1:18).

Well, that declaration which is made by the Evangelist is taken up and confirmed by Jesus himself, but with a fresh nuance. In fact, whereas John's Prologue speaks of an explanatory intervention by Jesus through the words of his teaching, in his answer to Philip Jesus refers to his own Person as such, letting it be understood that it is possible to understand him not only through his words but, rather, simply through what he is.

To express ourselves in accordance with the paradox of the Incarnation we can certainly say that God gave himself a human face, the Face of Jesus, and consequently, from now on, if we truly want to know the Face of God, all we have to do is to contemplate the Face of Jesus! In his Face we truly see who God is and what he looks like!

The Evangelist does not tell us whether Philip grasped the full meaning of Jesus' sentence. There is no doubt that he dedicated his whole life entirely to him. According to certain later accounts (*Acts of Philip* and others), our Apostle is said to have evangelized first Greece and then Frisia, where he is supposed to have died, in Hierapolis, by a torture described variously as crucifixion or stoning.

Let us conclude our reflection by recalling the aim to which our whole life must aspire: to encounter Jesus as Philip encountered him, seeking to perceive in him God himself, the heavenly Father. If this commitment were lacking, we would be reflected back to ourselves as in a mirror and become more and more lonely! Philip teaches us instead to let ourselves be won over by Jesus, to be with him and also to invite others to share in this indispensable company; and in seeing, finding God, to find true life.

19

Thomas the Twin

WEDNESDAY, 27 SEPTEMBER 2006
Saint Peter's Square

Dear Brothers and Sisters,

Continuing our encounters with the Twelve Apostles chosen directly by Jesus, today we will focus our attention on Thomas. Ever present in the four lists compiled by the New Testament, in the first three Gospels he is placed next to Matthew (cf. Mt 10:3; Mk 3:18; Lk 6:15), whereas in Acts, he is found after Philip (cf. Acts 1:13).

His name derives from a Hebrew root, *ta'am*, which means "paired, twin". In fact, John's Gospel several times calls him "Didymus" (cf. Jn 11:16; 20:24; 21:2), a Greek nickname for, precisely, "twin". The reason for this nickname is unclear.

It is above all the Fourth Gospel that gives us information that outlines some important traits of his personality.

The first concerns his exhortation to the other Apostles when Jesus, at a critical moment in his life, decided to go to Bethany to raise Lazarus, thus coming dangerously close to Jerusalem (Mk 10:32).

On that occasion Thomas said to his fellow disciples: "Let us also go, that we may die with him" (Jn 11:16). His determination to follow his Master is truly exemplary and offers us a valuable lesson: it reveals his total readiness to stand by Jesus, to the point of identifying his own destiny with that of Jesus and of desiring to share with him the supreme trial of death.

In fact, the most important thing is never to distance oneself from Jesus.

Moreover, when the Gospels use the verb "to follow", it means that where he goes, his disciple must also go.

Thus, Christian life is defined as a life with Jesus Christ, a life to spend together with him. Saint Paul writes something similar when he assures the Christians of Corinth: "You are in our hearts, to die together and to live together" (2 Cor 7:3). What takes place between the Apostle and his Christians must obviously apply first of all to the relationship between Christians and Jesus himself: dying together, living together, being in his Heart as he is in ours.

A second intervention by Thomas is recorded at the Last Supper. On that occasion, predicting his own imminent departure, Jesus announced that he was going to prepare a place for his disciples so that they could be where he is found; and he explains to them: "Where [I] am going you know the way" (Jn 14:4). It is then that Thomas intervenes, saying: "Lord, we do not know where you are going; how can we know the way?" (Jn 14:5).

In fact, with this remark he places himself at a rather low level of understanding; but his words provide Jesus with the opportunity to pronounce his famous definition: "I am the Way, and the Truth, and the Life" (Jn 14:6).

Thus, it is primarily to Thomas that he makes this revelation, but it is valid for all of us and for every age. Every time we hear or read these words, we can stand beside Thomas in spirit and imagine that the Lord is also speaking to us, just as he spoke to him.

At the same time, his question also confers upon us the right, so to speak, to ask Jesus for explanations. We often do not understand him. Let us be brave enough to say: "I do not understand you, Lord; listen to me, help me to understand." In such a way, with this frankness which is the true way of praying, of speaking to Jesus, we express our meager capacity to understand and at the same time place ourselves in the trusting attitude of someone who expects light and strength from the One able to provide them.

Then, the proverbial scene of the doubting Thomas that occurred eight days after Easter is very well known. At first he did not believe that Jesus had appeared in his absence and said: "Unless I see in his hands the print of the nails, and place my finger in the mark of the nails, and place my hand in his side, I will not believe" (Jn 20:25).

Basically, from these words emerges the conviction that Jesus can now be recognized by his wounds rather than by his face. Thomas holds that the signs that confirm Jesus' identity are now above all his wounds, in which he reveals to us how much he loved us. In this the Apostle is not mistaken.

As we know, Jesus reappeared among his disciples eight days later, and this time Thomas was present. Jesus summons him: "Put your finger here, and see my hands; and put out your hand, and place it in my side; do not be faithless, but believing" (Jn 20:27).

Thomas reacts with the most splendid profession of faith in the whole of the New Testament: "My Lord and my God!" (Jn 20:28). Saint Augustine comments on this: Thomas "saw and touched the man, and acknowledged the God whom he neither saw nor touched; but by the means of what he saw and touched, he now put far away from him every doubt, and believed the other" (*In ev. Jo.*, 121, 5).

The Evangelist continues with Jesus' last words to Thomas: "Have you believed because you have seen me? Blessed are those who have not seen and yet believe" (Jn 20:29). This sentence can also be put into the present: "Blessed are those who do not see and yet believe."

In any case, here Jesus spells out a fundamental principle for Christians who will come after Thomas, hence, for all of us.

It is interesting to note that another Thomas, the great Medieval theologian of Aquinas, juxtaposed this formula of blessedness with the apparently opposite one recorded by Luke: "Blessed are the eyes which see what you see!" (Lk 10:23). However, Aquinas comments: "Those who believe without seeing are more meritorious than those who, seeing, believe" (*In Johann.*, XX *lectio*, VI, 2566).

In fact, the Letter to the Hebrews, recalling the whole series of the ancient biblical Patriarchs who believed in God without seeing the fulfillment of his promises, defines faith as "the assurance of things hoped for, the conviction of things not seen" (Heb 11:1).

The Apostle Thomas' case is important to us for at least three reasons: first, because it comforts us in our insecurity; second, because it shows us that every doubt can lead to an outcome brighter than any uncertainty; and, lastly, because the words that Jesus addressed to him remind us of the true meaning of mature faith and encourage us to persevere, despite the difficulty, along our journey of adhesion to him.

A final point concerning Thomas is preserved for us in the Fourth Gospel, which presents him as a witness of the Risen One in the subsequent event of the miraculous catch in the Sea of Tiberias (cf. Jn 21:2ff.).

On that occasion, Thomas is even mentioned immediately after Simon Peter: an evident sign of the considerable importance that he enjoyed in the context of the early Christian communities.

Indeed, the *Acts* and the *Gospel of Thomas*, both apocryphal works but in any case important for the study of Christian origins, were written in his name.

Lastly, let us remember that an ancient tradition claims that Thomas first evangelized Syria and Persia (mentioned by Origen, according to Eusebius of Caesarea, *Hist. eccles.*, III, 1), then went on to Western India (cf. *Acts of Thomas*, 1–2 and 17ff.), from where also he finally reached Southern India.

Let us end our reflection in this missionary perspective, expressing the hope that Thomas' example will never fail to strengthen our faith in Jesus Christ, Our Lord and Our God.

20

Bartholomew

Dear Brothers and Sisters,

In the series on the Apostles called by Jesus during his earthly life, today it is the Apostle Bartholomew who attracts our attention. In the ancient lists of the Twelve he always comes before Matthew, whereas the name of the Apostle who precedes him varies; it may be Philip (cf. Mt 10:3; Mk 3:18; Lk 6:14) or Thomas (cf. Acts 1:13).

His name is clearly a patronymic, since it is formulated with an explicit reference to his father's name. Indeed, it is probably a name with an Aramaic stamp, *bar Talmay*, which means precisely: "son of Talmay".

We have no special information about Bartholomew; indeed, his name always and only appears in the lists of the Twelve mentioned above and is therefore never central to any narrative.

However, it has traditionally been identified with Nathanael: a name that means "God has given".

This Nathanael came from Cana (cf. Jn 21:2), and he may therefore have witnessed the great "sign" that Jesus worked in that place (cf. Jn 2:1–11). It is likely that the identification of the two figures stems from the fact that Nathanael is placed in the scene of his calling, recounted in John's Gospel, next to Philip, in other words, the place that Bartholomew occupies in the lists of the Apostles mentioned in the other Gospels.

Philip told this Nathanael that he had found "him of whom Moses in the law and also the prophets wrote, Jesus of Nazareth, the son of Joseph" (Jn 1:45). As we know, Nathanael's retort was rather strongly prejudiced: "Can anything good come out of Nazareth?" (Jn 1:46). In its own way, this form of protestation is important for us. Indeed, it makes us see that according to Judaic expectations the Messiah could not come from such an obscure village as, precisely, Nazareth (see also Jn 7:42).

But at the same time Nathanael's protest highlights God's freedom, which baffles our expectations by causing him to be found in the very place where we least expect him. Moreover, we actually know that Jesus was not exclusively "from Nazareth" but was born in Bethlehem (cf. Mt 2:1; Lk 2:4) and came ultimately from Heaven, from the Father who is in Heaven.

Nathanael's reaction suggests another thought to us: in our relationship with Jesus we must not be satisfied with words alone. In his answer, Philip offers Nathanael a meaningful invitation: "Come and see!" (Jn 1:46). Our knowledge of Jesus needs above all a first-hand experience: someone else's testimony is of course important, for normally the whole of our Christian life begins with the proclamation handed down to us by one or more witnesses.

However, we ourselves must then be personally involved in a close and deep relationship with Jesus; in a similar way, when the Samaritans had heard the testimony of their fellow citizen whom Jesus had met at Jacob's well, they wanted to talk to him directly, and after this conversation they told the woman: "It is no longer because of your words that we believe, for we have heard for ourselves, and we know that this is indeed the Savior of the world" (Jn 4:42).

Returning to the scene of Nathanael's vocation, the Evangelist tells us that when Jesus sees Nathanael approaching, he exclaims: "Behold, an Israelite indeed, in whom there is no guile!" (Jn 1:47). This is praise reminiscent of the text of a Psalm: "Blessed is the man . . . in whose spirit there is no deceit" (32[31]:2), but provokes the curiosity of Nathanael, who answers in amazement: "How do you know me?" (Jn 1:48).

Jesus' reply cannot immediately be understood. He says: "Before Philip called you, when you were under the fig tree, I saw you" (Jn 1:48). We do not know what had happened under this fig tree. It is obvious that it had to do with a decisive moment in Nathanael's life.

His heart is moved by Jesus' words; he feels understood and he understands: "This man knows everything about me, he knows and is familiar with the road of life; I can truly trust this man." And so he answers with a clear and beautiful confession of faith: "Rabbi, you are the Son of God! You are the King of Israel!" (Jn 1:49). In this confession is conveyed a first important step in the journey of attachment to Jesus.

Nathanael's words shed light on a twofold, complementary aspect of Jesus' identity: he is recognized both in his special relationship with God the Father, of whom he is the Only-begotten Son, and in his relationship with the People of Israel, of whom he is the declared King, precisely the description of the awaited Messiah. We must never lose sight of either of these two elements because if we only proclaim Jesus' heavenly dimension, we risk making him an ethereal and evanescent being; and if, on the contrary, we recognize only his concrete place in history, we end by neglecting the divine dimension that properly qualifies him.

We have no precise information about Bartholomew-Nathanael's subsequent apostolic activity. According to information handed down by Eusebius, the fourth-century historian, a certain Pantaenus is supposed to have discovered traces of Bartholomew's presence even in India (cf. *Hist. eccles.*, V, 10, 3).

In later tradition, as from the Middle Ages, the account of his death by flaying became very popular. Only think of the famous scene of the *Last Judgment* in the Sistine Chapel in which Michelangelo painted Saint Bartholomew, who is holding his own skin in his left hand, on which the artist left his self-portrait.

Saint Bartholomew's relics are venerated here in Rome in the Church dedicated to him on the Tiber Island, where they are said to have been brought by the German Emperor Otto III in the year 983.

To conclude, we can say that despite the scarcity of information about him, Saint Bartholomew stands before us to tell us that attachment to Jesus can also be lived and witnessed to without performing sensational deeds. Jesus himself, to whom each one of us is called to dedicate his own life and death, is and remains extraordinary.

21

Simon and Jude

Dear Brothers and Sisters,

Today, let us examine two of the Twelve Apostles: Simon the Cananaean and Jude Thaddaeus (not to be confused with Judas Iscariot). Let us look at them together, not only because they are always placed next to each other in the lists of the Twelve (cf. Mt 10:3, 4; Mk 3:18; Lk 6:15; Acts 1:13), but also because there is very little information about them, apart from the fact that the New Testament canon preserves one Letter attributed to Jude Thaddaeus.

Simon is given a nickname that varies in the four lists: while Matthew and Mark describe him as a "Cananaean", Luke instead describes him as a "Zealot".

In fact, the two descriptions are equivalent because they mean the same thing: indeed, in Hebrew the verb *qanà'* means "to be jealous, ardent" and can be said both of God, since he is jealous with regard to his Chosen People (cf. Ex 20:5), and of men who burn with zeal in serving the one God with unreserved devotion, such as Elijah (cf. 1 Kgs 19:10).

Thus, it is highly likely that even if this Simon was not exactly a member of the nationalist movement of Zealots, he was at least marked by passionate attachment to his Jewish identity, hence, for God, his People, and divine Law.

If this was the case, Simon was worlds apart from Matthew, who, on the contrary, had an activity behind him as a tax collector that was frowned upon as entirely impure. This shows that Jesus called his disciples and collaborators, without exception, from the most varied social and religious backgrounds.

It was people who interested him, not social classes or labels! And the best thing is that in the group of his followers, despite their differences, they all lived side by side, overcoming imaginable difficulties: indeed, what bound them together was Jesus himself, in whom they all found themselves united with one another.

This is clearly a lesson for us who are often inclined to accentuate differences and even contrasts, forgetting that in Jesus Christ we are given the strength to get the better of our continual conflicts.

Let us also bear in mind that the group of the Twelve is the prefiguration of the Church, where there must be room for all charisms, peoples, and races, all human qualities that find their composition and unity in communion with Jesus.

Then with regard to Jude Thaddaeus, this is what tradition has called him, combining two different names: in fact, whereas Matthew and Mark call him simply "Thaddaeus" (Mt 10:3; Mk 3:18), Luke calls him "Judas, the son of James" (Lk 6:16; Acts 1:13).

The nickname "Thaddaeus" is of uncertain origin and is explained either as coming from the Aramaic *taddà'*, which means "breast" and would therefore suggest "magnanimous", or as an abbreviation of a Greek name, such as "Teodòro, Teòdoto".

Very little about him has come down to us. John alone mentions a question he addressed to Jesus at the Last Supper: Thaddaeus says to the Lord: "Lord, how is it that you will manifest yourself to us and not to the world?"

This is a very timely question which we also address to the Lord: why did not the Risen One reveal himself to his enemies in his full glory in order to show that it is God who is victorious? Why did he manifest himself only to his disciples? Jesus' answer is mysterious and profound. The Lord says: "If a man loves me, he will keep my word, and my Father will love him, and we will come to him and make our home with him" (Jn 14:22–23).

This means that the Risen One must be seen, must be perceived also by the heart, in a way so that God may take up his abode within us. The Lord does not appear as a thing. He desires to enter our lives, and therefore his manifestation is a manifestation that implies and presupposes an open heart. Only in this way do we see the Risen One.

The paternity of one of those New Testament Letters known as "catholic", since they are not addressed to a specific local Church but intended for a far wider circle, has been attributed to Jude Thaddaeus. Actually, it is addressed "to those who are called, beloved in God the Father and kept for Jesus Christ" (v. 1).

A major concern of this writing is to put Christians on guard against those who make a pretext of God's grace to excuse their own licentiousness and corrupt their brethren with unacceptable teachings, introducing division within the Church "in their dreamings" (v. 8).

This is how Jude defines their doctrine and particular ideas. He even compares them to fallen angels and, mincing no words, says that "they walk in the way of Cain" (v. 11).

Furthermore, he brands them mercilessly as "waterless clouds, carried along by winds; fruitless trees in late autumn, twice dead, uprooted; wild waves of the sea, casting up the foam of their own shame; wandering stars for whom the nether gloom of darkness has been reserved for ever" (vv. 12–13).

Today, perhaps, we are no longer accustomed to using language that is so polemic, yet that tells us something important. In the midst of all the temptations that exist, with all the currents of modern life, we must preserve our faith's identity. Of course, the way of indulgence and dialogue, on which the Second Vatican Council happily set out, should certainly be followed firmly and consistently.

But this path of dialogue, while so necessary, must not make us forget our duty to rethink and to highlight just as forcefully the main and indispensable aspects of our Christian identity. Moreover, it is essential to keep clearly in mind that our identity requires strength, clarity, and courage in light of the contradictions of the world in which we live.

Thus, the text of the Letter continues: "But you, beloved"— he is speaking to all of us—"build yourselves up on your most holy faith; pray in the Holy Spirit; keep yourselves in the love of God; wait for the mercy of our Lord Jesus Christ unto eternal life. And convince some, who doubt . . ." (vv. 20–22).

The Letter ends with these most beautiful words: "To him who is able to keep you from falling and to present you without blemish before the presence of his glory with rejoicing, to the only God, our Savior through Jesus Christ our Lord, be glory, majesty, dominion and authority, before all time and now and for ever. Amen" (vv. 24–25).

It is easy to see that the author of these lines lived to the full his own faith, to which realities as great as moral integrity and joy, trust, and lastly praise belong, since it is all motivated solely by the goodness of our one God and the mercy of our Lord Jesus Christ.

Therefore, may both Simon the Cananaean and Jude Thaddeus help us to rediscover the beauty of the Christian faith ever anew and to live it without tiring, knowing how to bear a strong and at the same time peaceful witness to it.

22

Judas Iscariot and Matthias

Dear Brothers and Sisters,

Today, concluding our walk through the portrait gallery of the Apostles called directly by Jesus during his earthly life, we cannot fail to mention the one who has always been named last in the list of the Twelve: Judas Iscariot. We want to associate him with the person who is later elected to substitute for him, Matthias.

Already the very name of Judas raises among Christians an instinctive reaction of criticism and condemnation.

The meaning of the name "Judas" is controversial: the more common explanation considers him as a "man from Kerioth", referring to his village of origin situated near Hebron and mentioned twice in Sacred Scripture (cf. Gn 15:25; Am 2:2). Others interpret it as a variant of the term "hired assassin", as if to allude to a warrior armed with a dagger, in Latin, *sica*.

Lastly, there are those who see in the label a simple inscription of a Hebrew-Aramaic root meaning: "the one who is to hand him over". This designation is found twice in the Gospel: after Peter's confession of faith (cf. Jn 6:71) and then in the course of the anointing at Bethany (cf. Jn 12:4).

Another passage shows that the betrayal was under way, saying: "he who betrayed him"; and also during the Last

Supper, after the announcement of the betrayal (cf. Mt 26:25), and then at the moment of Jesus' arrest (cf. Mt 26:46, 48; Jn 18:2, 5). Rather, the lists of the Twelve recalls the fact of the betrayal as already fulfilled: "Judas Iscariot, who betrayed him", says Mark (3:19); Matthew (10:4) and Luke (6:16) have equivalent formulas.

The betrayal itself happens in two moments: before all, in the planning, when Judas agreed with Jesus' enemies to thirty pieces of silver (cf. Mt 26:14–16), and then, in its execution, with the kiss given to the Master in Gethsemane (cf. Mt 26:46–50).

In any case, the Evangelists insist on the status as an Apostle that Judas held in all regards: he is repeatedly called "one of the twelve" (Mt 26:14, 47; Mk 14:10, 20; Jn 6:71) or "of the number of the twelve" (Lk 22:3).

Moreover, on two occasions, Jesus, addressing the Apostles and speaking precisely of Judas, indicates him as "one of you" (Mt 26:21; Mk 14:18; Jn 6:70; 13:21). And Peter will say of Judas that "he was numbered among us and allotted his share in this ministry" (Acts 1:17).

He is therefore a figure belonging to the group of those whom Jesus had chosen as strict companions and collaborators. This brings with it two questions in the attempt to provide an explanation for what happened.

The first consists in asking how is it that Jesus had chosen this man and trusted him. In fact, although Judas is the group's bursar (cf. Jn 12:6b; 13:29a), in reality he is called a "thief" (Jn 12:6a).

The mystery of the choice remains, all the more since Jesus pronounces a very severe judgment on him: "Woe to that man by whom the Son of man is betrayed!" (Mt 26:24).

What is more, it darkens the mystery around his eternal fate, knowing that Judas "repented and brought back the thirty pieces of silver to the chief priests and the elders, saying, 'I have sinned in betraying innocent blood'" (Mt 27:3–4). Even though he went to hang himself (cf. Mt 27:5), it is not up to us to judge his gesture, substituting ourselves for the infinitely merciful and just God.

A second question deals with the motive of Judas' behavior: why does he betray Jesus? The question raises several theories. Some refer to the fact of his greed for money; others hold to an explanation of a messianic order: Judas would have been disappointed at seeing that Jesus did not fit into his program for the political–militaristic liberation of his own nation.

In fact, the Gospel texts insist on another aspect: John expressly says that "the devil had already put it into the heart of Judas Iscariot, Simon's son, to betray him" (Jn 13:2). Analogously, Luke writes: "Then Satan entered into Judas called Iscariot, who was of the number of the twelve" (Lk 22:3).

In this way, one moves beyond historical motivations and explanations based on the personal responsibility of Judas, who shamefully ceded to a temptation of the Evil One.

The betrayal of Judas remains, in any case, a mystery. Jesus treated him as a friend (cf. Mt 26:50); however, in his invitations to follow him along the way of the beatitudes, he does not force his will or protect it from the temptations of Satan, respecting human freedom.

In effect, the possibilities to pervert the human heart are truly many. The only way to prevent it consists in not cultivating an individualistic, autonomous vision of things, but on the contrary, by putting oneself always on the side of Jesus, assuming his point of view. We must daily seek to build full communion with him.

Let us remember that Peter also wanted to oppose him and

what awaited him at Jerusalem, but he received a very strong
reproval: "You are not on the side of God, but of men" (Mk
8:33)!

After his fall Peter repented and found pardon and grace.
Judas also repented, but his repentance degenerated into
desperation and thus became self-destructive.

For us it is an invitation always to remember what Saint
Benedict says at the end of the fundamental Chapter Five of
his "Rule": "Never despair of God's mercy." In fact, God "is
greater than our hearts", as Saint John says (1 Jn 3:20).

Let us remember two things. The first: Jesus respects our
freedom. The second: Jesus awaits our openness to repentance and conversion; he is rich in mercy and forgiveness.

Besides, when we think of the negative role Judas played
we must consider it according to the lofty ways in which God
leads events. His betrayal led to the death of Jesus, who
transformed this tremendous torment into a space of salvific
love by consigning himself to the Father (cf. Gal 2:20; Eph
5:2, 25).

The word "to betray" is the version of a Greek word that
means "to consign". Sometimes the subject is even God in
person: it was he who for love "consigned" Jesus for all of us
(Rom 8:32). In his mysterious salvific plan, God assumes
Judas' inexcusable gesture as the occasion for the total gift of
the Son for the redemption of the world.

In conclusion, we want to remember the one who, after
Easter, was elected in place of the betrayer. In the Church of
Jerusalem two were proposed to the community, and then
lots were cast for their names: "Joseph called Barsabbas, who
was surnamed Justus, and Matthias" (Acts 1:23).

Precisely the latter was chosen; hence, "he was enrolled
with the eleven apostles" (Acts 1:26). We know nothing else
about him, except that he had been a witness to all Jesus'

earthly events (cf. Acts 1:21–22), remaining faithful to him to the end. To the greatness of his fidelity was later added the divine call to take the place of Judas, almost compensating for his betrayal.

We draw from this a final lesson: while there is no lack of unworthy and traitorous Christians in the Church, it is up to each of us to counterbalance the evil done by them with our clear witness to Jesus Christ, our Lord and Savior.

23

Paul of Tarsus

WEDNESDAY, 25 OCTOBER 2006
Saint Peter's Square

Dear Brothers and Sisters,

We have concluded our reflections on the Twelve Apostles, called directly by Jesus during his earthly life. Today, we begin to examine the figures of other important early Church personalities.

They also spent their lives for the Lord, the Gospel, and the Church. They are men and also women who, as Luke writes in the Book of Acts, "have risked their lives for the sake of Our Lord Jesus Christ" (15:26).

The first of these, called by the Lord himself, by the Risen One, to be a true Apostle, is undoubtedly Paul of Tarsus. He shines like a star of the brightest magnitude in the Church's history, and not only in that of her origins. Saint John Chrysostom praised him as a person superior even to many angels and archangels (cf. *Panegirico*, 7, 3). Dante Alighieri in the *Divine Comedy*, inspired by Luke's account in Acts (cf. 9:15), describes him simply as "vessel of election" (*Inf.* 2:28), which means: instrument chosen by God. Others called him the "thirteenth Apostle", or directly, "the first after the Only".

Certainly, after Jesus, he is one of the originals of whom we have the most information. In fact, we possess not only the account that Luke gives in the Acts of the Apostles, but also a group of Letters that have come directly from his hand

and which, without intermediaries, reveal his personality and thought.

Luke tells us that his name originally was Saul (cf. Acts 7:58; 8:1), in Hebrew also Saul (cf. Acts 9:14, 17; 22:7, 13; 26:14), like King Saul (cf. Acts 13:21), and he was a Jew of the diaspora, since the city of Tarsus is situated between Anatolia and Syria.

Very soon he went to Jerusalem to study the roots of Mosaic Law in the footsteps of the great Rabbi Gamaliel (cf. Acts 22:3). He also learned a manual and common trade, tent making (cf. Acts 18:3), which later permitted him to provide personally for his own support without being a weight on the Churches (cf. Acts 20:34; 1 Cor 4:12; 2 Cor 12:13).

It was decisive for him to know the community of those who called themselves disciples of Jesus. Through them he came to know a new faith—a new "way", as it was called— that places not so much the Law of God at the center but rather the person of Jesus, Crucified and Risen, to whom was now linked the remission of sins. As a zealous Jew, he held this message unacceptable, even scandalous, and he therefore felt the duty to persecute the followers of Christ even outside of Jerusalem.

It was precisely on the road to Damascus at the beginning of the 30s A.D. that, according to his words, "Christ made me his own" (Phil 3:12). While Luke recounts the fact with abundant detail—like how the light of the Risen One touched him and fundamentally changed his whole life—in his Letters he goes directly to the essential and speaks not only of a vision (cf. 1 Cor 9:1), but of an illumination (cf. 2 Cor 4:6), and above all of a revelation and of a vocation in the encounter with the Risen One (cf. Gal 1:15–16).

In fact, he will explicitly define himself as "apostle by vocation" (cf. Rom 1:1; 1 Cor 1:1) or "apostle by the will of God" (2 Cor 1:1; Eph 1:1; Col 1:1), as if to emphasize that his conversion was not the result of a development of thought or reflection, but the fruit of divine intervention, an unforeseeable, divine grace.

Henceforth, all that had constituted for him a value paradoxically became, according to his words, a loss and refuse (cf. Phil 3:7–10). And from that moment all his energy was placed at the exclusive service of Jesus Christ and his Gospel. His existence would become that of an Apostle who wants to "become all things to all men" (1 Cor 9:22) without reserve.

From here we draw a very important lesson: what counts is to place Jesus Christ at the center of our lives, so that our identity is marked essentially by the encounter, by communion with Christ and with his Word. In his light every other value is recovered and purified from possible dross.

Another fundamental lesson offered by Paul is the universal breadth that characterizes his apostolate. Acutely feeling the problem of the Gentiles, of the pagans, to know God, who in Jesus Christ Crucified and Risen offers salvation to all without exception, he dedicates himself to make this Gospel— literally, "good news"—known, to announce the grace destined to reconcile men with God, self, and others.

From the first moment he understood that this is a reality that did not concern only the Jews or a certain group of men, but one that had a universal value and concerned everyone, because God is the God of everyone.

The point of departure for his travels was the Church of Antioch in Syria, where for the first time the Gospel was announced to the Greeks and where also the name "Christians" was coined (cf. Acts 11:20, 26), believers in Christ.

From there he first went to Cyprus and then on different occasions to the regions of Asia Minor (Pisidia, Laconia, Galatia), and later to those of Europe (Macedonia, Greece).

The most famous were the cities of Ephesus, Philippi, Thessalonica, Corinth, without forgetting Berea, Athens, and Miletus.

In Paul's apostolate difficulties were not lacking, which he faced with courage for love of Christ. He himself recalls having endured

> labors . . . imprisonment . . . beatings . . . numerous brushes with death. . . . Three times I was beaten with rods, once I was stoned, three times I was shipwrecked, I passed a night and a day on the deep; on frequent journeys, in dangers from rivers, dangers from robbers, dangers from my own race, dangers from Gentiles, dangers in the city, dangers in the wilderness, dangers at sea, dangers among false brothers; in toil and hardship, through many sleepless nights, through hunger and thirst, through frequent fastings, cold and exposure. And apart from these things there is the daily pressure upon me of my anxiety for all the Churches. (2 Cor 11:23–28)

From a passage of the Letter to the Romans (cf. 15:24, 28) appears his proposal to push on even to Spain, to the Far West, to announce the Gospel everywhere, even to the then known ends of the earth. How can one not admire a man like this? How can one not thank the Lord for having given an Apostle of this stature?

It is clear that he would not have been able to face such difficult and at times desperate situations if he did not have a reason of absolute value, before which no limit could be considered insurmountable. For Paul, this reason, as we know, is Jesus Christ, of whom he writes: "The love of Christ impels us . . . so that those who live might live no longer for themselves but for him who for their sake died and was raised" (2 Cor 5:14–15), for us, for all.

In fact, the Apostle renders the supreme witness of blood

under the Emperor Nero here in Rome, where we keep and venerate his mortal remains. Clement of Rome, my Predecessor to this Apostolic See, wrote of him in the last years of the first century: "Because of jealousy and discord, Paul was obliged to show us how one obtains the prize of patience. . . . After preaching justice to all in the world, and after having arrived at the limits of the West, he endured martyrdom before the political rulers; in this way he left this world and reached the holy place, thus becoming the greatest model of perseverance" (*To the Corinthians*, 5).

May the Lord help us to put into practice the exhortation left to us by the Apostle in his Letters: "Be imitators of me, as I am of Christ" (1 Cor 11:1).

24

Saint Paul's New Outlook

WEDNESDAY, 8 NOVEMBER 2006
Saint Peter's Square

Dear Brothers and Sisters,

In our previous Catechesis two weeks ago, I endeavored to sketch the essential lines of the biography of the Apostle Paul. We saw how his encounter with Christ on the road to Damascus literally revolutionized his life. Christ became his *raison d'être* and the profound motivation of all his apostolic work.

In his Letters, after the Name of God, which appears more than five hundred times, the name most frequently mentioned is Christ's (380 times). Thus, it is important to realize what a deep effect Jesus Christ can have on a person's life, hence, also on our own lives. Actually, the history of salvation culminates in Jesus Christ, and thus he is also the true discriminating point in the dialogue with other religions.

Looking at Paul, this is how we could formulate the basic question: how does a human being's encounter with Christ occur? And of what does the relationship that stems from it consist? The answer given by Paul can be understood in two stages.

In the first place, Paul helps us to understand the absolutely basic and irreplaceable value of faith. This is what he wrote in his Letter to the Romans: "We hold that a man is justified by faith apart from works of law" (3:28).

This is what he also wrote in his Letter to the Galatians: "[M]an is not justified by works of the law but only through faith in Jesus Christ; even we have believed in Christ Jesus, in order to be justified by faith in Christ, and not by works of the law, because by works of the law shall no one be justified" (2:16).

"Being justified" means being made righteous, that is, being accepted by God's merciful justice to enter into communion with him and, consequently, to be able to establish a far more genuine relationship with all our brethren: and this takes place on the basis of the complete forgiveness of our sins.

Well, Paul states with absolute clarity that this condition of life does not depend on our possible good works but on the pure grace of God: "[We] are justified by his grace as a gift, through the redemption which is in Christ Jesus" (Rom 3:24). With these words Saint Paul expressed the fundamental content of his conversion, the new direction his life took as a result of his encounter with the Risen Christ.

Before his conversion, Paul had not been a man distant from God and from his Law. On the contrary, he had been observant, with an observance faithful to the point of fanaticism. In the light of the encounter with Christ, however, he understood that with this he had sought to build up himself and his own justice, and that with all this justice he had lived for himself.

He realized that a new approach in his life was absolutely essential. And we find this new approach expressed in his words: "The life I now live in the flesh I live by faith in the Son of God, who loved me and gave himself for me" (Gal 2:20).

Paul, therefore, no longer lives for himself, for his own justice. He lives for Christ and with Christ: in giving of himself, he is no longer seeking and building himself up. This is the new justice, the new orientation given to us by the Lord, given to us by faith.

Before the Cross of Christ, the extreme expression of his self-giving, there is no one who can boast of himself, of his own self-made justice, made for himself! Elsewhere, re-echoing Jeremiah, Paul explains this thought, writing, "Let him who boasts, boast of the Lord" (1 Cor 1:31 = Jer 9:23–24ff.); or: "Far be it from me to glory except in the Cross of Our Lord Jesus Christ, by which the world has been crucified to me, and I to the world" (Gal 6:14).

In reflecting on what justification means, not for actions but for faith, we thus come to the second component that defines the Christian identity described by Saint Paul in his own life.

This Christian identity is composed of precisely two elements: this restraint from seeking oneself by oneself but instead receiving oneself from Christ and giving oneself with Christ, thereby participating personally in the life of Christ himself to the point of identifying with him and sharing both his death and his life. This is what Paul wrote in his Letter to the Romans: "[A]ll of us . . . were baptized into his death . . . we were buried therefore with him . . . we have been united with him. . . . So you also must consider yourselves dead to sin and alive to God in Christ Jesus" (Rom 6:3, 4, 5, 11).

These last words themselves are symptomatic: for Paul, in fact, it was not enough to say that Christians are baptized or believers; for him, it was just as important to say they are "in Christ Jesus" (cf. also Rom 8:1, 2, 39; 12:5; 16:3, 7, 10; 1 Cor 1:2, 3, etc.).

At other times he inverted the words and wrote: "Christ is in us/you" (Rom 8:10; 2 Cor 13:5) or "in me" (Gal 2:20).

This mutual compenetration between Christ and the Christian, characteristic of Paul's teaching, completes his discourse on faith.

In fact, although faith unites us closely to Christ, it emphasizes the distinction between us and him; but according to Paul, Christian life also has an element that we might describe as "mystical", since it entails an identification of ourselves with Christ and of Christ with us. In this sense, the Apostle even went so far as to describe our suffering as "the suffering of Christ" in us (2 Cor 1:5), so that we might "always [carry] in the body the death of Jesus, so that the life of Jesus may also be manifested in our bodies" (2 Cor 4:10).

We must fit all this into our daily lives by following the example of Paul, who always lived with this great spiritual range. Besides, faith must constantly express humility before God, indeed, adoration and praise.

Indeed, it is to him and his grace alone that we owe what we are as Christians. Since nothing and no one can replace him, it is necessary that we pay homage to nothing and no one else but him. No idol should pollute our spiritual universe, or otherwise, instead of enjoying the freedom acquired, we will relapse into a humiliating form of slavery.

Moreover, our radical belonging to Christ and the fact that "we are in him" must imbue in us an attitude of total trust and immense joy. In short, we must indeed exclaim with Saint Paul: "If God is for us, who is against us?" (Rom 8:31). And the reply is that nothing and no one "will be able to separate us from the love of God in Christ Jesus our Lord" (Rom 8:39). Our Christian life, therefore, stands on the soundest and safest rock one can imagine. And from it we draw all our energy, precisely as the Apostle wrote: "I can do all things in him who strengthens me" (Phil 4:13).

Therefore, let us face our life with its joys and sorrows supported by these great sentiments that Paul offers to us. By having an experience of them we will realize how true are the words the Apostle himself wrote: "I know whom I have believed, and I am sure that he is able to guard until that Day what has been entrusted to me"; in other words, until the Day (2 Tm 1:12) of our definitive meeting with Christ the Judge, Savior of the world and our Savior.

25

Saint Paul and the Spirit

WEDNESDAY, 15 NOVEMBER 2006
Saint Peter's Square

Dear Brothers and Sisters,

Today too, as in our last two Catecheses, we return to Saint Paul and his thought. We have before us a giant, not only in terms of his actual apostolate but also of his extraordinarily profound and stimulating theological teaching.

After meditating last time on what Paul wrote about the central place that Jesus Christ occupies in our life of faith, today let us look at what he said about the Holy Spirit and about his presence in us, because here too, the Apostle has something very important to teach us.

We know what Saint Luke told us of the Holy Spirit from his description of the event of Pentecost in the Acts of the Apostles. The Spirit of Pentecost brought with him a strong impulse to take on the commitment of the mission in order to witness to the Gospel on the highways of the world.

Indeed, the Acts of the Apostles relates a whole series of missions the Apostles carried out, first in Samaria, then on the coastal strip of Palestine, then towards Syria. Above all, the three great missionary journeys of Paul are recounted, as I recalled at one of our previous Wednesday meetings.

In his Letters, however, Saint Paul also spoke to us of the Spirit from another angle. He did not end by describing solely the dynamic and active dimension of the Third Person of the Blessed Trinity, but also analyzed his presence in the lives of Christians, which marks their identity.

In other words, in Paul's reflection on the Spirit he explained his influence not only on the *action* of Christians, but also on their *being*. Indeed, it is he who said that the Spirit of God dwells in us (cf. Rom 8:9; 1 Cor 3:16) and that "God has sent the Spirit of his Son into our hearts" (Gal 4:6).

In Paul's opinion, therefore, the Spirit stirs us to the very depths of our being. Here are some of his words on this subject which have an important meaning: "For the law of the Spirit of life in Christ Jesus has set me free from the law of sin and death . . . you did not receive the spirit of slavery to fall back into fear, but you have received the spirit of sonship. When we cry, 'Abba! Father!', it is the Spirit himself" (Rom 8:2, 15) who speaks in us because, as children, we can call God "Father".

Thus, we can see clearly that even before he does anything, the Christian already possesses a rich and fruitful interiority, given to him in the Sacraments of Baptism and Confirmation, an interiority which establishes him in an objective and original relationship of sonship with God. This is our greatest dignity: to be not merely images but also children of God. And it is an invitation to live our sonship, to be increasingly aware that we are adoptive sons in God's great family. It is an invitation to transform this objective gift into a subjective reality, decisive for our way of thinking, acting, and being.

God considers us his children, having raised us to a similar if not equal dignity to that of Jesus himself, the one true Son in the full sense. Our filial condition and trusting freedom in our relationship with the Father is given or restored to us in him.

We thus discover that for Christians, the Spirit is no longer only the "Spirit of God", as he is usually described in the Old Testament and as people continue to repeat in Christian language (cf. Gn 41:38; Ex 31:3; 1 Cor 2:11, 12; Phil 3:3; etc.). Nor is he any longer simply a "Holy Spirit" generically understood, in the manner of the Old Testament (cf. Is 63:10, 11; Ps 51[50]:13), and of Judaism itself in its writings (Qumran, rabbinism).

Indeed, the confession of an original sharing in this Spirit by the Risen Lord, who himself became a "life-giving Spirit" (1 Cor 15:45), is part of the specificity of the Christian faith.

For this very reason, Saint Paul spoke directly of the "Spirit of Christ" (Rom 8:9), of the "Spirit of his Son" (cf. Gal 4:6), or of the "Spirit of Jesus Christ" (Phil 1:19). It is as though he wanted to say that not only is God the Father visible in the Son (cf. Jn 14:9), but that the Spirit of God also expresses himself in the life and action of the Crucified and Risen Lord!

Paul teaches us another important thing: he says that there is no true prayer without the presence of the Spirit within us. He wrote: "The Spirit helps us in our weakness; for we do not know how to pray as we ought, but the Spirit himself intercedes for us with sighs too deep for words. And he who searches the hearts of men knows what is the mind of the Spirit, because the Spirit intercedes for the saints according to the will of God" (Rom 8:26–27).

It is as if to say that the Holy Spirit, that is, the Spirit of the Father and of the Son, is henceforth as it were the soul of our soul, the most secret part of our being, from which an impulse of prayer rises ceaselessly to God, whose words we cannot even begin to explain.

In fact, the Spirit, ever alert within us, completes what is lacking in us and offers to the Father our worship as well as our deepest aspirations.

This, of course, requires a degree of great and vital communion with the Spirit. It is an invitation to be increasingly sensitive, more attentive to this presence of the Spirit in us, to transform it into prayer, to feel this presence and thus to learn to pray, to speak to the Father as children in the Holy Spirit.

There is also another typical aspect of the Spirit which Saint Paul teaches us: his connection with love. Thus, the Apostle wrote: "Hope does not disappoint us, because God's love has been poured into our hearts through the Holy Spirit who has been given to us" (Rom 5:5).

In my Encyclical Letter *Deus Caritas Est*, I cited a most eloquent sentence of Saint Augustine: "If you see charity, you see the Trinity" (no. 19), and I continued by explaining: "The Spirit, in fact, is that interior power which harmonizes [believers'] hearts with Christ's heart and moves them to love their brethren as Christ loved them" (*ibid.*). The Spirit immerses us in the very rhythm of divine life, which is a life of love, enabling us to share personally in relations between the Father and the Son. It is not without significance that when Paul lists the various elements that constitute the fruit of the Spirit he puts love first: "the fruit of the Spirit is love, joy, peace", etc. (Gal 5:22).

And since by definition, love unites, this means first of all that the Spirit is the creator of communion within the Christian community, as we say at the beginning of Mass, borrowing Paul's words: ". . . may the fellowship of the Holy Spirit [that is, what he brings about] be with you all" (2 Cor 13:14).

Furthermore, however, it is also true that the Spirit stimulates us to weave charitable relations with all people. Therefore, when we love we make room for the Spirit and give him leeway to express himself fully within us.

We thus understand why Paul juxtaposes in the same passage of his Letter to the Romans the two exhortations: "Be aglow with the Spirit" and "Repay no one evil for evil" (Rom 12:11, 17).

Finally, according to Saint Paul, the Spirit is a generous down payment given to us by God himself as a deposit and, at the same time, a guarantee of our future inheritance (cf. 2 Cor 1:22; 5:5; Eph 1:13–14).

We therefore learn from Paul that the Spirit's action directs our life towards the great values of love, joy, communion, and hope. It is our task to experience this every day, complying with the inner promptings of the Spirit and helped in our discernment by the Apostle's enlightened guidance.

26

Saint Paul and the Church

WEDNESDAY, 22 NOVEMBER 2006

Saint Peter's Square

Dear Brothers and Sisters,

Today, we are ending our encounters with the Apostle Paul by dedicating one last reflection to him. Indeed, we cannot take our leave of him without considering one of the decisive elements of his activity and one of the most important subjects of his thought: the reality of the Church.

We must first of all note that his initial contact with the Person of Jesus happened through the witness of the Christian community of Jerusalem. It was a turbulent contact. Having met the new group of believers, he immediately became a fierce persecutor of it. He acknowledged this himself at least three times in as many of his Letters: "I persecuted the Church of God" (1 Cor 15:9; Gal 1:13; Phil 3:6), as if to describe his behavior as the worst possible crime.

History shows us that one usually reaches Jesus by passing through the Church! In a certain sense, this proved true, we were saying, also for Paul, who encountered the Church before he encountered Jesus. In his case, however, this contact was counterproductive; it did not result in attachment but violent rejection.

For Paul, adherence to the Church was brought about by a direct intervention of Christ, who in revealing himself on the road to Damascus identified himself with the Church and made Paul realize that persecution of the Church was persecution of himself, the Lord.

In fact, the Risen One said to Paul, persecutor of the Church: "Saul, Saul, why do you persecute me?" (Acts 9:4). In persecuting the Church, he was persecuting Christ.

Paul, therefore, was at the same time converted to Christ and to the Church. This leads one to understand why the Church later became so present in Paul's thoughts, heart, and activity.

In the first place, she was so present that he literally founded many Churches in the various cities where he went as an evangelizer. When he spoke of his "anxiety for all the Churches" (2 Cor 11:28), he was thinking of the various Christian communities brought into being from time to time in Galatia, Ionia, Macedonia, and in Achaea.

Some of those Churches also caused him worry and chagrin, as happened, for example, in the Churches of Galatia, which he saw "turning to a different gospel" (Gal 1:6), something he opposed with grim determination.

Yet, he felt bound to the Communities he founded in a way that was far from cold and bureaucratic but rather intense and passionate. Thus, for example, he described the Philippians as "my brethren, whom I love and long for, my joy and crown" (Phil 4:1).

On other occasions he compared the various Communities to a letter of recommendation, unique in its kind: "You yourselves are our letter of recommendation, written on your hearts, to be known and read by all men" (2 Cor 3:2).

At yet other times, he showed a real feeling for them that was not only paternal but also maternal, such as when he turned to those he was addressing, calling them: "My little children, with whom I am again in travail until Christ be formed in you" (Gal 4:19; cf. also 1 Cor 4:14–15; 1 Thes 2:7–8).

Paul also illustrates for us in his Letters his teaching on the Church as such. Thus, his original definition of the Church as the "Body of Christ", which we do not find in other Christian authors of the first century, is well known (cf. 1 Cor 12:27; Eph 4:12; 5:30; Col 1:24).

We find the deepest root of this surprising designation of the Church in the Sacrament of the Body of Christ. Saint Paul said: "Because there is one bread, we who are many are one body" (1 Cor 10:17). In the same Eucharist, Christ gives us his Body and makes us his Body. Concerning this, Saint Paul said to the Galatians: "You are all one in Christ" (Gal 3:28). By saying all this, Paul makes us understand that not only does the belonging of the Church to Christ exist, but also a certain form of equality and identification of the Church with Christ himself.

From this, therefore, derive the greatness and nobility of the Church, that is, of all of us who are part of her: from our being members of Christ, an extension as it were of his personal presence in the world. And from this, of course, stems our duty truly to live in conformity with Christ.

Paul's exhortations concerning the various charisms that give life and structure to the Christian community also derive from this. They can all be traced back to a single source, that is, the Spirit of the Father and of the Son, knowing well that in the Church there is no one who goes without them, for, as the Apostle wrote, "to each is given the manifestation of the Spirit for the common good" (1 Cor 12:7).

It is important, however, that all the charisms cooperate with one another for the edification of the community and do not instead become the cause of a rift.

In this regard, Paul asked himself rhetorically: "Is Christ

divided?" (1 Cor 1:13). He knows well and teaches us that it is necessary to "maintain the unity of the Spirit in the bond of peace. There is one body and one Spirit, just as you were called to the one hope that belongs to your call" (Eph 4:3–4).

Obviously, underlining the need for unity does not mean that ecclesial life should be standardized or leveled out in accordance with a single way of operating. Elsewhere, Paul taught: "Do not quench the Spirit" (1 Thes 5:19), that is, make room generously for the unforeseeable dynamism of the charismatic manifestations of the Spirit, who is an ever new source of energy and vitality.

But if there is one tenet to which Paul stuck firmly it was mutual edification: "Let all things be done for edification" (1 Cor 14:26). Everything contributes to weaving the ecclesial fabric evenly, not only without slack patches but also without holes or tears.

Then, there is also a Pauline Letter that presents the Church as Christ's Bride (cf. Eph 5:21–33).

With this, Paul borrowed an ancient prophetic metaphor which made the People of Israel the Bride of the God of the Covenant (cf. Hos 2:4, 21; Is 54:5–8). He did so to express the intimacy of the relationship between Christ and his Church, both in the sense that she is the object of the most tender love on the part of her Lord, and also in the sense that love must be mutual and that we too therefore, as members of the Church, must show him passionate faithfulness.

Thus, in short, a relationship of communion is at stake: the so to speak *vertical* communion between Jesus Christ and all of us, but also the *horizontal* communion between all who are distinguished in the world by the fact that they "call on the name of Our Lord Jesus Christ" (1 Cor 1:2).

This is our definition: we belong among those who call on the Name of the Lord Jesus Christ. Therefore, we clearly understand how desirable it is that what Paul himself was hoping for when he wrote to the Corinthians should come to pass: "If an unbeliever or an uninitiated enters while all are uttering prophecy, he will be taken to task by all and called to account by all, and the secret of his heart will be laid bare. Falling prostrate, he will worship God, crying out, 'God is truly among you'" (1 Cor 14:24–25).

Our liturgical encounters should be like this. A non-Christian who enters one of our assemblies ought finally to be able to say: "God is truly with you." Let us pray to the Lord to be like this, in communion with Christ and in communion among ourselves.

27

Timothy and Titus

WEDNESDAY, 13 DECEMBER 2006
Paul VI Audience Hall

Dear Brothers and Sisters,

Having spoken at length on the great Apostle Paul, today let us look at his two closest collaborators: Timothy and Titus. Three Letters traditionally attributed to Paul are addressed to them, two to Timothy and one to Titus.

Timothy is a Greek name which means "one who honors God". Whereas Luke mentions him six times in the Acts, Paul in his Letters refers to him at least seventeen times (and his name occurs once in the Letter to the Hebrews).

One may deduce from this that Paul held him in high esteem, even if Luke did not consider it worth telling us all about him.

Indeed, the Apostle entrusted Timothy with important missions and saw him almost as an *alter ego*, as is evident from his great praise of him in his Letter to the Philippians. "I have no one like him (*isópsychon*) who will be genuinely anxious for your welfare" (2:20).

Timothy was born at Lystra (about two hundred kilometers northwest of Tarsus) of a Jewish mother and a Gentile father (cf. Acts 16:1).

The fact that his mother had contracted a mixed-marriage and did not have her son circumcised suggests that Timothy grew up in a family that was not strictly observant, although it was said that he was acquainted with the Scriptures from childhood (cf. 2 Tm 3:15). The name of his mother, Eunice, has been handed down to us as well as that of his grandmother, Lois (cf. 2 Tm 1:5).

When Paul was passing through Lystra at the beginning of his second missionary journey, he chose Timothy to be his companion because "he was well spoken of by the brethren at Lystra and Iconium" (Acts 16:2), but he had him circumcised "because of the Jews that were in those places" (Acts 16:3).

Together with Paul and Silas, Timothy crossed Asia Minor as far as Troy, from where he entered Macedonia. We are informed further that at Philippi, where Paul and Silas were falsely accused of disturbing public order and thrown into prison for having exposed the exploitation of a young girl who was a soothsayer by several unscrupulous individuals (cf. Acts 16:16–40), Timothy was spared.

When Paul was then obliged to proceed to Athens, Timothy joined him in that city and from it was sent out to the young Church of Thessalonica to obtain news about her and to strengthen her in the faith (cf. 1 Thes 3:1–2). He then met up with the Apostle in Corinth, bringing him good news about the Thessalonians and working with him to evangelize that city (cf. 2 Cor 1:19).

We find Timothy at Ephesus during Paul's third missionary journey. It was probably from there that the Apostle wrote to Philemon and to the Philippians; he sent both Letters jointly with Timothy (cf. Phlm 1; Phil 1:1).

From Ephesus, Paul sent Timothy to Macedonia, together with a certain Erastus (cf. Acts 19:22), and then also to Corinth with the mission of taking a letter to the Corinthians, in which he recommended that they welcome him warmly (cf. 1 Cor 4:17; 16:10–11).

We encounter him again as the joint sender of the Second Letter to the Corinthians, and when Paul wrote the Letter to the Romans from Corinth he added Timothy's greetings as well as the greetings of the others (cf. Rom 16:21).

From Corinth, the disciple left for Troy on the Asian coast of the Aegean See and there awaited the Apostle, who was bound for Jerusalem at the end of his third missionary journey (cf. Acts 20:4).

From that moment in Timothy's biography, the ancient sources mention nothing further to us, except for a reference in the Letter to the Hebrews which says: "You should understand that our brother Timothy has been released, with whom I shall see you if he comes soon" (13:23).

To conclude, we can say that the figure of Timothy stands out as a very important pastor.

According to the later *Ecclesiastical History* by Eusebius, Timothy was the first Bishop of Ephesus (cf. *Hist. eccles.*, III, 4). Some of his relics, brought from Constantinople, were found in Italy in 1239 in the Cathedral of Termoli in the Molise.

Then, as regards the figure of *Titus*, whose name is of Latin origin, we know that he was Greek by birth, that is, a pagan (cf. Gal 2:3). Paul took Titus with him to Jerusalem for the so-called Apostolic Council, where the preaching of the Gospel to the Gentiles that freed them from the constraints of Mosaic Law was solemnly accepted.

In the Letter addressed to Titus, the Apostle praised him and described him as his "true child in a common faith" (Ti 1:4). After Timothy's departure from Corinth, Paul sent Titus there with the task of bringing that unmanageable community to obedience.

Titus restored peace between the Church of Corinth and the Apostle, who wrote to this Church in these terms: "But

God, who comforts the downcast, comforted us by the coming of Titus, and not only by his coming but also by the comfort with which he was comforted in you, as he told us of your longing, your mourning, your zeal for me. . . . And besides our own comfort we rejoiced still more at the joy of Titus, because his mind has been set at rest by you all" (2 Cor 7:6–7, 13).

From Corinth, Titus was again sent out by Paul—who called him "my partner and fellow worker in your service" (2 Cor 8:23)—to organize the final collections for the Christians of Jerusalem (cf. 2 Cor 8:6).

Further information from the Pastoral Letters describes him as Bishop of Crete (cf. Ti 1:5), from which, at Paul's invitation, he joined the Apostle at Nicopolis in Epirus (cf. Ti 3:12). Later, he also went to Dalmatia (cf. 2 Tm 4:10). We lack any further information on the subsequent movements of Titus or on his death.

To conclude, if we consider together the two figures of Timothy and Titus, we are aware of certain very significant facts. The most important one is that in carrying out his missions, Paul availed himself of collaborators. He certainly remains the Apostle par excellence, founder and pastor of many Churches.

Yet it clearly appears that he did not do everything on his own but relied on trustworthy people who shared in his endeavors and responsibilities.

Another observation concerns the willingness of these collaborators. The sources concerning Timothy and Titus highlight their readiness to take on various offices that also often consisted in representing Paul in circumstances far from easy. In a word, they teach us to serve the Gospel with generosity, realizing that this also entails a service to the Church herself.

Lastly, let us follow the recommendation that the Apostle Paul makes to Titus in the Letter addressed to him: "I desire you to insist on these things, so that those who have believed in God may be careful to apply themselves to good deeds; these are excellent and profitable to men" (Ti 3:8).

Through our commitment in practice we can and must discover the truth of these words, and precisely in this Season of Advent, we too can be rich in good deeds and thus open the doors of the world to Christ, our Savior.

28

Stephen, the Protomartyr

WEDNESDAY, 10 JANUARY 2007

Dear Brothers and Sisters,

After the period of festivity, we return to our Catecheses. I
have meditated with you on the figures of the Twelve
Apostles and on Saint Paul. We then began to reflect on other
figures of the newborn Church, and so let us consider today
the person of Saint Stephen, whom the Church commemo-
rates the day after Christmas.

Saint Stephen is the most representative of a group of
seven companions. Tradition sees in this group the seed of
the future ministry of "deacons", although it must be pointed
out that this category is not present in the Book of Acts. In
any case, Stephen's importance is due to the fact that Luke, in
his important book, dedicates two whole chapters to him.

Luke's narrative starts with the observation of a widespread
division in the primitive Church of Jerusalem: indeed, she
consisted entirely of Christians of Jewish origin, but some
came from the land of Israel and were called "Hebrews",
while others, of the Old Testament Jewish faith, came from
the Greek-speaking diaspora and were known as "Hellenists". This was the new problem: the most destitute of the
Hellenists, especially widows deprived of any social support,
ran the risk of being neglected in the daily distribution of
their rations. To avoid this problem, the Apostles, continuing
to devote themselves to prayer and the ministry of the Word,

decided to appoint for this duty "seven men of good repute, full of the Spirit and of wisdom" to help them (Acts 6:2–4), that is, by carrying out a social and charitable service.

To this end, as Luke wrote, at the Apostles' invitation the disciples chose seven men. We are even given their names. They were: "Stephen, a man full of faith and of the Holy Spirit, Philip, Prochorus, Nicanor, Timon, Parmenas and Nicolaus. These they set before the Apostles, and they prayed and laid their hands upon them" (cf. Acts 6:5–6).

The act of the laying on of hands can have various meanings. In the Old Testament, this gesture meant above all the transmission of an important office, just as Moses laid his hands on Joshua (cf. Nm 27:18–23), thereby designating his successor. Along the same lines, the Church of Antioch would also use this gesture in sending out Paul and Barnabas on their mission to the peoples of the world (cf. Acts 13:3).

The two Pauline Letters addressed to Timothy (cf. 1 Tm 4:14; 2 Tm 1:6) refer to a similar imposition of hands on Timothy, to confer upon him an official responsibility. From what we read in the First Letter to Timothy, we can deduce that this was an important action to be carried out after discernment: "Do not be hasty in the laying on of hands, nor participate in another man's sins" (5:22).

Thus, we see that the act of the laying on of hands developed along the lines of a sacramental sign. In the case of Stephen and his companions, it was certainly an official conferral of an office by the Apostles, but at the same time an entreaty for the grace to carry it out.

The most important thing to note is that in addition to charitable services, Stephen also carried out a task of evangelization among his compatriots, the so-called "Hellenists". Indeed, Luke insists on the fact that Stephen, "full of grace and power" (Acts 6:8), presented in Jesus' Name a new interpretation of Moses and of God's Law itself. He reread the Old Testament in the light of the proclamation of Christ's death and Resurrection. He gave the Old Testament a Christological reinterpretation and provoked reactions from the Jews, who took his words to be blasphemous (cf. Acts 6:11–14).

For this reason he was condemned to stoning. And Saint Luke passes on to us the saint's last discourse, a synthesis of his preaching. Just as Jesus had shown the disciples of Emmaus that the whole of the Old Testament speaks of him, of his Cross and his Resurrection, so Saint Stephen, following Jesus' teaching, interpreted the whole of the Old Testament in a Christological key. He shows that the mystery of the Cross stands at the center of the history of salvation as recounted in the Old Testament; it shows that Jesus, Crucified and Risen, is truly the goal of all this history.

Saint Stephen also shows that the cult of the Temple was over and that Jesus, the Risen One, was the new, true "temple". It was precisely this "no" to the Temple and to its cult that led to the condemnation of Saint Stephen, who at this moment, Saint Luke tells us, gazed into Heaven and saw the glory of God, and Jesus standing at the right hand of God, and seeing Heaven, God, and Jesus, Saint Stephen said, "Behold, I see the heavens opened, and the Son of man standing at the right hand of God" (cf. Acts 7:56).

This was followed by his martyrdom, modeled in fact on the Passion of Jesus himself, since he delivered his own spirit to the "Lord Jesus" and prayed that the sin of those who killed him would not be held against them (cf. Acts 7:59–60).

The place of Saint Stephen's martyrdom in Jerusalem has traditionally been located outside the Damascus Gate, to the north, where indeed the Church of Saint-Étienne [Saint Stephen] stands beside the famous *École Biblique* of the

Dominicans. The killing of Stephen, the first martyr of Christ, unleashed a local persecution of Christ's disciples (cf. Acts 8:1), the first one in the history of the Church. It was these circumstances that impelled the group of Judeo-Hellenist Christians to flee from Jerusalem and scatter. Hounded out of Jerusalem, they became itinerant missionaries: "Those who were scattered went about preaching the word" (Acts 8:4).

Their persecution and consequent dispersion became a mission. Thus, the Gospel spread also to Samaria, Phoenicia, and Syria, as far as the great city of Antioch, where, according to Luke, it was proclaimed for the first time also to the pagans (cf. Acts 11:19–20) and where, for the first time, the name "Christians" was used (Acts 11:26).

In particular, Luke noted that those who stoned Stephen "laid down their garments at the feet of a young man named Saul" (Acts 7:58), the same man who from being a persecutor was to become an outstanding Apostle of the Gospel.

This means that the young Saul must have heard Stephen's preaching and must therefore have been acquainted with its principal content. And Saint Paul was probably among those who, following and listening to this discourse, "were enraged and . . . ground their teeth against him" (Acts 7:54).

And at this point, we can see the marvels of divine Providence. After his encounter with the Risen Christ on the road to Damascus, Saul, a relentless enemy of Stephen's vision, took up the Christological interpretation of the Old Testament made by the First Martyr, deepening and completing it, and consequently became the "Apostle to the Gentiles".

The Law is fulfilled, he taught, in the Cross of Christ. And faith in Christ, communion with Christ's love, is the true fulfillment of all the Law. This is the content of Paul's preaching. He showed in this way that the God of Abraham had become the God of all. And all believers in Jesus Christ, as children of Abraham, shared in the promises. Saint Stephen's vision was brought about in Saint Paul's mission.

Stephen's story tells us many things: for example, that charitable social commitment must never be separated from the courageous proclamation of the faith. He was one of the seven made responsible above all for charity. But it was impossible to separate charity and faith. Thus, with charity, he proclaimed the crucified Christ, to the point of accepting even martyrdom. This is the first lesson we can learn from the figure of Saint Stephen: charity and the proclamation of faith always go hand in hand.

Above all, Saint Stephen speaks to us of Christ, of the Crucified and Risen Christ as the center of history and our life. We can understand that the Cross remains forever the center of the Church's life and also of our life. In the history of the Church, there will always be passion and persecution. And it is persecution itself which, according to Tertullian's famous words, becomes "the seed of Christians", the source of mission for Christians to come.

I cite his words: "We multiply wherever we are mown down by you: the blood of Christians is seed . . ." (*Apology*, 50, 13): *plures efficimur quoties metimur a vobis: semen est sanguis christianorum.* But in our life, too, the Cross that will never be absent becomes a blessing.

And by accepting our cross, knowing that it becomes and is a blessing, we learn Christian joy even in moments of difficulty. The value of witness is irreplaceable, because the Gospel leads to it and the Church is nourished by it. Saint Stephen teaches us to treasure these lessons; he teaches us to love the Cross, because it is the path on which Christ comes among us ever anew.

Barnabas, Silas (Also Called Silvanus), and Apollos

WEDNESDAY, 31 JANUARY 2007

Dear Brothers and Sisters,

Continuing our journey among the protagonists who were the first to spread Christianity, today let us turn our attention to some of Saint Paul's other collaborators. We must recognize that the Apostle is an eloquent example of a man open to collaboration: he did not want to do everything in the Church on his own but availed himself of many and very different colleagues.

We cannot reflect on all these precious assistants because they were numerous. It suffices to recall, among others, Epaphras (cf. Col 1:7; 4:12; Phlm 23), Epaphroditus (cf. Phil 2:25; 4:18), Tychicus (cf. Acts 20:4; Eph 6:21; Col 4:7; 2 Tm 4:12; Ti 3:12), Urbanus (cf. Rom 16:9), Gaius and Aristarchus (cf. Acts 19:29; 20:4; 27:2; Col 4:10). And women such as Phoebe (Rom 16:1), Tryphaena and Tryphosa (cf. Rom 16:12), Persis, the mother of Rufus, whom Paul called "his mother and mine" (cf. Rom 16:12–13), not to mention married couples such as Prisca and Aquila (cf. Rom 16:3; 1 Cor 16:19; 2 Tm 4:19).

Among this great array of Saint Paul's male and female collaborators, let us focus today on three of these people who played a particularly significant role in the initial evangelization: Barnabas, Silas, and Apollos.

Barnabas means "son of encouragement" (Acts 4:36) or "son of consolation". He was a Levite Jew, a native of Cyprus, and this was his nickname. Having settled in Jerusalem, he was one of the first to embrace Christianity after the Lord's Resurrection. With immense generosity, he sold a field which belonged to him and gave the money to the Apostles for the Church's needs (Acts 4:37).

It was he who vouched for the sincerity of Saul's conversion before the Jerusalem community that still feared its former persecutor (cf. Acts 9:27).

Sent to Antioch in Syria, he went to meet Paul in Tarsus, where he had withdrawn, and spent a whole year with him there, dedicated to the evangelization of that important city in whose Church Barnabas was known as a prophet and teacher (cf. Acts 13:1).

At the time of the first conversions of the Gentiles, therefore, Barnabas realized that Saul's hour had come. As Paul had retired to his native town of Tarsus, he went there to look for him. Thus, at that important moment, Barnabas, as it were, restored Paul to the Church; in this sense he gave back to her the Apostle to the Gentiles.

The Church of Antioch sent Barnabas on a mission with Paul, which became known as the Apostle's first missionary journey. In fact, it was Barnabas' missionary voyage since it was he who was really in charge of it and Paul had joined him as a collaborator, visiting the regions of Cyprus and Central and Southern Anatolia in present-day Turkey, with the cities of Attalia, Perga, Antioch of Pisidia, Iconium, Lystra, and Derbe (cf. Acts 13–14).

Together with Paul, he then went to the so-called Council of Jerusalem, where after a profound examination of the question, the Apostles with the Elders decided to discontinue the practice of circumcision so that it was no longer a feature of the Christian identity (cf. Acts 15:1–35). It was only in this way that, in the end, they officially made possible the Church of the Gentiles, a Church without circumcision; we are children of Abraham simply through faith in Christ.

The two, Paul and Barnabas, disagreed at the beginning of the second missionary journey because Barnabas was determined to take with them as a companion John called Mark, whereas Paul was against it, since the young man had deserted them during their previous journey (cf. Acts 13:13; 15:36–40).

Hence there are also disputes, disagreements, and controversies among saints. And I find this very comforting, because we see that the saints have not "fallen from Heaven". They are people like us, who also have complicated problems.

Holiness does not consist in never having erred or sinned. Holiness increases the capacity for conversion, for repentance, for willingness to start again, and, especially, for reconciliation and forgiveness.

So it was that Paul, who had been somewhat harsh and bitter with regard to Mark, in the end found himself with him once again. In Saint Paul's last Letters, to Philemon and in his Second Letter to Timothy, Mark actually appears as one of his "fellow workers".

Consequently, it is not the fact that we have never erred but our capacity for reconciliation and forgiveness which makes us saints. And we can all learn this way of holiness. In any case, Barnabas, together with John Mark, returned to Cyprus (Acts 15:39) in about the year 49. From that moment we lose track of him. Tertullian attributes to him the Letter to the Hebrews. This is not improbable. Since he belonged to the tribe of Levi, Barnabas may have been interested in the topic of the priesthood; and the Letter to the Hebrews interprets Jesus' priesthood for us in an extraordinary way.

Silas was another of Paul's companions. "Silas" is a Greek form of a Jewish name (perhaps *sheal*, "to ask, to invoke", which has the same root as the name "Saul"); from which the Latin form *Sylvanus* also derives. The name Silas is attested to only in the Book of Acts, while the name "Silvanus" appears only in the Pauline Letters. He was a Jew from Jerusalem, one of the first to become a Christian, and he enjoyed high esteem in that Church (cf. Acts 15:22), since he was considered a prophet (cf. Acts 15:32).

He was charged to inform "the brethren who are of the Gentiles in Antioch and Syria and Cilicia" (Acts 15:23) of the decisions taken at the Council of Jerusalem and to explain them. Evidently he was considered capable of bringing about a sort of mediation between Jerusalem and Antioch, between Jewish-Christians and Christians of pagan origin and thereby of serving the unity of the Church in the diversity of rites and origins.

When Paul separated from Barnabas he took Silas with him as his new traveling companion (Acts 15:40). With Paul, he reached Macedonia (and the cities of Philippi, Thessalonica, and Beroea), where he stopped, while Paul went on to Athens and then to Corinth.

Silas joined him in Corinth, where he cooperated in preaching the Gospel; indeed, in the Second Letter that Paul addressed to that Church, he spoke of "Jesus Christ, whom we preached among you, Silvanus and Timothy and I" (2 Cor 1:19). This explains how he came to be the joint author, together with Paul and Timothy, of the two Letters to the Thessalonians.

This also seems important to me. Paul does not act as a "soloist", on his own, but together with these collaborators in the "we" of the Church. This "I" of Paul is not an isolated "I" but an "I" in the "we" of the Church, in the "we" of the apostolic faith. And later, Silvanus is also mentioned in the First Letter of Peter, in which we read: "I have written [briefly] to you . . . by Silvanus, a faithful brother" (5:12). Thus, we also see the communion of the Apostles. Silvanus serves Paul and he serves Peter, because the Church is one and the missionary proclamation is one.

Paul's third companion whom we want to recall is Apollos. This name is probably an abbreviation of Apollonius or Apollodorus. Although this is a pagan name, he was a fervent Jew from Alexandria, Egypt. Luke, in the book of the Acts of the Apostles, describes him as "an eloquent man, well versed in the Scriptures . . . fervent in spirit" (18:24–25).

Apollos' entry on the scene of the first evangelization took place in the city of Ephesus. He had gone there to preach and had the good fortune to come across the Christian couple Priscilla and Aquila, who introduced him to a fuller knowledge of the "way of God" (cf. Acts 18:26).

From Ephesus he went to Achaia and reached the city of Corinth, where he arrived with a letter of recommendation from the Christians of Ephesus, in which they charged the Corinthians to give him a good welcome (cf. Acts 18:27). In Corinth, as Luke wrote: "he greatly helped those who through grace had believed, for he powerfully confuted the Jews in public, showing by the Scriptures that the Christ was Jesus" (Acts 18:27–28), the Messiah.

His success in that city, however, had a problematic sequence [downside] since there were certain members of that Church who, fascinated by his way of speaking, opposed the others in his name (cf. 1 Cor 1:12; 3:4–6; 4:6).

In his First Letter to the Corinthians, Paul expressed his appreciation of Apollos' work, but reprimanded the

Corinthians for wounding the Body of Christ by splitting it into opposing factions. From this whole affair he drew an important teaching: be it I or Apollos, he says, we are none other than *diakonoi*, that is, simple ministers, through whom you have come to the faith (cf. 1 Cor 3:5).

Everyone has a different task in the field of the Lord: "I planted, Apollos watered, but God gave the growth. . . . [W]e are God's fellow workers; you are God's field, God's building" (1 Cor 3:6–9).

After returning to Ephesus, Apollos resisted Paul's invitation to return to Corinth immediately, postponing the journey to a later date of which we know nothing (cf. 1 Cor 16:12). We have no further information about him, even though some scholars believe he is a possible author of the Letter to the Hebrews which Tertullian believed Barnabas had written.

These three men shine in the firmament of Gospel witnesses as they are distinguished by one common feature as well as by individual characteristics. They had in common, in addition to their Jewish origin, their dedication to Jesus Christ and the Gospel, besides the fact that all three were collaborators of the Apostle Paul.

In this original evangelizing mission they found their purpose in life and as such stand before us as shining examples of selflessness and generosity.

Moreover, let us think again of Saint Paul's phrase: both Apollos and I are servants of Jesus, each one in his own way because it is God who gives the growth. These words also apply to us today, to the Pope, the Cardinals, Bishops, priests, and laity. We are all humble ministers of Jesus. We serve the Gospel as best we can, in accordance with our talents, and we pray God to make his Gospel, his Church, increase in our day.

30

Priscilla and Aquila

WEDNESDAY, 7 FEBRUARY 2007

Dear Brothers and Sisters,

Taking a new step in this type of portrait gallery of the first witnesses of the Christian faith which we began some weeks ago, today we take into consideration a married couple.

The couple in question are Priscilla and Aquila, who take their place, as we already mentioned briefly last Wednesday, in the sphere of numerous collaborators who gravitated around the Apostle Paul. Based on the information in our possession, this married couple played a very active role in the post-Paschal origins of the Church.

The names Aquila and Priscilla are Latin, but the man and woman who bear them were of Hebrew origin. At least Aquila, however, geographically came from the diaspora of northern Anatolia, which faces the Black Sea—in today's Turkey—while Priscilla was probably a Jewish woman from Rome (cf. Acts 18:2).

However, it was from Rome that they reached Corinth, where Paul met them at the beginning of the 50s. There he became associated with them, as Luke tells us, practicing the same trade of making tents or large draperies for domestic use, and he was even welcomed into their home (cf. Acts 18:3).

The reason they came to Corinth was the decision taken by the Emperor Claudius to expel from Rome the city's

Jewish residents. Concerning this event the Roman historian
Suetonius tells us that the Hebrews were expelled because
"they were rioting due to someone named Chrestus" (cf.
"The Lives of the Twelve Caesars, Claudius", no. 25).

One sees that he did not know the name well—instead of
Christ he wrote "Chrestus"—and he had only a very confused idea of what had happened. In any case, there were
internal discords within the Jewish community about the
question if Jesus was the Christ. And for the Emperor these
problems were the reason simply to expel all Jews from
Rome.

One can deduce that the couple had already embraced the
Christian faith in the 40s, and now they had found in Paul
someone who not only shared with them this faith—that
Jesus is the Christ—but was also an Apostle, personally called
by the Risen Lord.

Therefore, their first encounter is at Corinth, where they
welcomed him into their house and worked together making
tents.

In a second moment they transferred to Ephesus in Asia
Minor. There they had a decisive role in completing the
Christian formation of the Alexandrian Jew Apollo, about
whom we spoke last Wednesday.

Since he only knew the faith superficially, "Priscilla and
Aquila . . . took him and expounded to him the way of God
more accurately" (Acts 18:26).

When Paul wrote the First Letter to the Corinthians from
Ephesus, together with his own greeting he explicitly sent
those of "Aquila and Prisca, together with the church in their
house" (16:19).

Hence, we come to know the most important role that this
couple played in the environment of the primitive Church:
that of welcoming in their own house the group of local

Christians when they gathered to listen to the Word of God and to celebrate the Eucharist. It is exactly this type of gathering that in Greek is called *ekklesía*—the Latin word is *ecclesia*, the Italian *chiesa*—which means convocation, assembly, gathering.

In the house of Aquila and Priscilla, therefore, the Church gathered, the convocation of Christ, which celebrates here the Sacred Mysteries.

Thus, we can see the very birth of the reality of the Church in the homes of believers. Christians, in fact, from the first part of the third century did not have their own places of worship. Initially it was the Jewish Synagogue, until the original symbiosis between the Old and New Testaments dissolved and the Church of the Gentiles was forced to give itself its own identity, always profoundly rooted in the Old Testament.

Then, after this "break", they gathered in the homes of Christians that thus become "Church". And finally, in the third century, true and proper buildings for Christian worship were born.

But here, in the first half of the first century and in the second century, the homes of Christians become a true and proper "Church". As I said, together they read the Sacred Scripture and celebrate the Eucharist.

That was what used to happen, for example, at Corinth, where Paul mentioned a certain "Gaius, who is host to me and to the whole church" (Rom 16:23), or at Laodicea, where the community gathered in the home of a certain Nympha (cf. Col 4:15), or at Colossae, where the meeting took place in the house of a certain Archippus (cf. Phlm 2).

Having returned subsequently to Rome, Aquila and Priscilla continue to carry out this precious function also in the capital of the Empire.

In fact, Paul, writing to the Romans, sends this precise greeting: "Greet Prisca and Aquila, my fellow workers in Christ Jesus, who risked their necks for my life, to whom not only I but also all the churches of the Gentiles give thanks; greet also the church in their house" (Rom 16:3–5).

What extraordinary praise for these two married persons in these words! And it is none other than Paul who extends it. He explicitly recognizes in them two true and important collaborators of his apostolate.

The reference made to having risked their lives for him is probably linked to interventions in his favor during some prison stay, perhaps in the same Ephesus (cf. Acts 19:23; 1 Cor 15:32; 2 Cor 1:8–9). And to Paul's own gratitude even that of all the Churches of the Gentiles is joined. Even if the expression is perhaps somewhat hyperbolic, it lets one intuit how vast the radius of their action was and, therefore, their influence for the good of the Gospel.

Later hagiographic tradition has given a very singular importance to Priscilla, even if the problem of identifying her with the martyr Priscilla remains.

In any case, here in Rome we have a Church dedicated to Saint Prisca on the Aventine Hill, near the Catacombs of Priscilla on Via Salaria.

In this way, the memory of a woman who has certainly been an active person and of great value in the history of Roman Christianity is perpetuated. One thing is sure: together with the gratitude of the early Church, of which Saint Paul speaks, we must also add our own, since thanks to the faith and apostolic commitment of the lay faithful, of families, of spouses like Priscilla and Aquila, Christianity has reached our generation.

It could not grow only due to the Apostles who announced it. In order to take root in people's land and develop actively, the commitment of these families, these spouses, these Christian communities, of these lay faithful was necessary in order to offer the "humus" for the growth of the faith. As always, it is only in this way that the Church grows.

This couple in particular demonstrates how important the action of Christian spouses is. When they are supported by the faith and by a strong spirituality, their courageous commitment for the Church and in the Church becomes natural. The daily sharing of their life prolongs and in some way is sublimated in the assuming of a common responsibility in favor of the Mystical Body of Christ, even if just a little part of it. Thus it was in the first generation and thus it will often be.

A further lesson we cannot neglect to draw from their example: every home can transform itself into a little church. Not only in the sense that in them must reign the typical Christian love made of altruism and of reciprocal care, but still more in the sense that the whole of family life, based on faith, is called to revolve around the singular lordship of Jesus Christ.

Not by chance does Paul compare, in the Letter to the Ephesians, the matrimonial relationship to the spousal communion that happens between Christ and the Church (cf. Eph 5:25–33). Even more, we can maintain that the Apostle indirectly models the life of the entire Church on that of the family. And the Church, in reality, is the family of God.

Therefore, we honor Aquila and Priscilla as models of conjugal life responsibly committed to the service of the entire Christian community. And we find in them the model of the Church, God's family for all times.

31

Women at the Service of the Gospel

WEDNESDAY, 14 FEBRUARY 2007

Paul VI Audience Hall

Dear Brothers and Sisters,

Today, we have come to the end of our journey among the witnesses of early Christianity mentioned in the New Testament writings. And we use the last step of this first journey to dedicate our attention to the many female figures who played an effective and precious role in spreading the Gospel.

In conformity with what Jesus himself said of the woman who anointed his head shortly before the Passion: "Truly, I say to you, wherever this Gospel is preached in the whole world, what she has done will be told in memory of her" (Mt 26:13; Mk 14:9), their testimony cannot be forgotten.

The Lord wants these Gospel witnesses, these figures who have made a contribution so that faith in him would grow, to be known and their memory kept alive in the Church. We can historically distinguish the role of the first women in early Christianity, during Jesus' earthly life and in the events of the first Christian generation.

Jesus, as we know, certainly chose from among his disciples twelve men as Fathers of the new Israel and appointed them "to be with him, and to be sent out to preach" (Mk 3:14–15).

This fact is obvious; but, in addition to the Twelve, pillars of the Church and Fathers of the new People of God, many women were also chosen to number among the disciples. I can only mention very briefly those who followed Jesus himself, beginning with the Prophetess Anna (cf. Lk 2:36–38), to the Samaritan woman (cf. Jn 4:1–39), the Syro-Phoenician woman (cf. Mk 7:24–30), the woman with the hemorrhage (cf. Mt 9:20–22), and the sinful woman whose sins were forgiven (cf. Lk 7:36–50).

I will not even refer to the protagonists of some of his effective parables, for example, the housewife who made bread (cf. Mt 13:33), the woman who lost the drachma (cf. Lk 15:8–10), the widow who pestered the judge (cf. Lk 18:1–8). More important for our topic are the women who played an active role in the context of Jesus' mission.

In the first place, we think spontaneously of the Virgin Mary, who with her faith and maternal labors collaborated in a unique way in our Redemption to the point that Elizabeth proclaimed her "Blessed . . . among women" (Lk 1:42), adding: "Blessed is she who believed . . ." (Lk 1:45).

Having become a disciple of her Son, Mary manifested total trust in him at Cana (cf. Jn 2:5) and followed him to the foot of the Cross, where she received from him a maternal mission for all his disciples of all times, represented by John (cf. Jn 19:25–27).

Then there are various women with roles of responsibility who gravitated in their different capacities around the figure of Jesus. The women who followed Jesus to assist him with their own means, some of whose names Luke has passed down to us, are an eloquent example: Mary of Magdala, Joanna, Susanna, and "many others" (cf. Lk 8:2–3).

The Gospels then tell us that the women, unlike the Twelve, did not abandon Jesus in the hour of his Passion (cf. Mt 27:56, 61; Mk 15:40). Among them, Mary Magdalene stands out in particular. Not only was she present at the

Passion, but she was also the first witness and herald of the Risen One (cf. Jn 20:1, 11–18).

It was precisely to Mary Magdalene that Saint Thomas Aquinas reserved the special title, "Apostle of the Apostles" (*apostolorum apostola*), dedicating to her this beautiful comment: "Just as a woman had announced the words of death to the first man, so also a woman was the first to announce to the Apostles the words of life" (*Super Ioannem*, ed. Cai, 2519).

Nor was the female presence in the sphere of the primitive Church in any way secondary. We will not insist on the four unnamed daughters of Philip the "Deacon" who lived at Caesarea; they were all endowed with the "gift of prophecy", as Saint Luke tells us, that is, the faculty of intervening publicly under the action of the Holy Spirit (cf. Acts 21:9). The brevity of information does not permit more precise deductions.

It is rather to Saint Paul that we are indebted for a more ample documentation on the dignity and ecclesial role of women. He begins with the fundamental principle according to which for the baptized: "There is neither Jew nor Greek, there is neither slave nor free, there is neither male nor female; for you are all one in Christ Jesus" (Gal 3:28), that is, all are united in the same basic dignity, although each with specific functions (cf. 1 Cor 12:27–30).

The Apostle accepts as normal the fact that a woman can "prophesy" in the Christian community (1 Cor 11:5), that is, speak openly under the influence of the Spirit, as long as it is for the edification of the community and done in a dignified manner.

Thus, the following well-known exhortation: "Women should keep silence in the Churches" (1 Cor 14:34) is instead to be considered relative. Let us leave to the exegetes the consequent, much discussed problem of the relationship

between the first phrase—women can prophesy in Churches—and the other—they are not permitted to speak; that
is, the relationship between these two apparently contradictory instructions. This is not for discussion here.

Last Wednesday we already came across the figure of Prisca
or Priscilla, Aquila's wife, who surprisingly is mentioned
before her husband in two cases (cf. Acts 18:18; Rom 16:3):
in any case, both are explicitly described by Paul as his *sun-
ergoús*, "collaborators" (Rom 16:3).

There are several other important points that cannot be
ignored. It should be noted, for example, that Paul's short
Letter to Philemon is actually also addressed to a woman
called "Apphia" (cf. Phlm 2). The Latin and Syriac translations of the Greek text add to this name, "Apphia", the
appellative "*soror carissima*" (*ibid.*), and it must be said that she
must have held an important position in the community at
Colossae. In any case, she is the only woman mentioned by
Paul among those to whom he addressed a Letter.

Elsewhere, the Apostle mentions a certain "Phoebe", described as "a deaconess of the Church at Cenchreae", the
port town east of Corinth (Rom 16:1–2). Although at that
time the title had not yet acquired a specific ministerial
value of a hierarchical kind, it expresses a true and proper
exercise of responsibility on the part of this woman for this
Christian community. Paul recommends that she be received cordially and assisted "in whatever she may require".
Then he adds: "for she has been a helper of many and of
myself as well".

In the same epistolary context the Apostle outlines with
delicate touches the names of other women: a certain Mary,
then Tryphaena, Tryphosa, and "the beloved" Persis, as well
as Julia, of whom he writes openly that they have "worked
hard among you" or "worked hard in the Lord" (Rom 16:6,

12a, 12b, 15), thereby emphasizing their strong ecclesial commitment.

Furthermore, in the Church at Philippi two women were to distinguish themselves, Euodia and Syntyche (cf. Phil 4:2). Paul's entreaty to mutual agreement suggests that these two women played an important role in that community.

In short, without the generous contribution of many women, the history of Christianity would have developed very differently.

This is why, as my venerable and dear Predecessor John Paul II wrote in his Apostolic Letter *Mulieris Dignitatem*: "The Church gives thanks for each and every woman. . . . The Church gives thanks for all the manifestations of the feminine 'genius' which have appeared in the course of history, in the midst of all peoples and nations; she gives thanks for all the charisms which the Holy Spirit distributes to women in the history of the People of God, for all the victories which she owes to their faith, hope, and charity: she gives thanks for all the fruits of feminine holiness" (no. 31).

As we can see, the praise refers to women in the course of the Church's history and was expressed on behalf of the entire Ecclesial Community. Let us also join in this appreciation, thanking the Lord because he leads his Church, generation after generation, availing himself equally of men and women who are able to make their faith and Baptism fruitful for the good of the entire Ecclesial Body and for the greater glory of God.

SCRIPTURE INDEX

OLD TESTAMENT

Genesis

12	43
15:25	104
17:5	50
22	43
32:28ff.	50
41:38	121

Exodus

20:5	100
31:3	121

Leviticus

19:18	74

Numbers

27:18–23	135

1 Kings

19:10	100

Psalms

32[31]:2	98
51[50]:13	121

Isaiah

54:5–8	127
63:10–11	121

Jeremiah

9:23–24ff.	116

Ezekiel

34:22–24	14
37:15–19	9
39:21	15
39:23–29	9
40–48	9

Hosea

2:4	127
2:21	127

Amos

2:2	104

NEW TESTAMENT

Matthew

2:1	97
4:13	82
4:18–22	12
4:18–19	54
4:19	7, 12
4:20	59
4:21	67
5:46	82
7:17	66
8:14ff.	40
9:1–8	82
9:9	81
9:10	82
9:20–22	151
10:1–4	9, 54
10:2–3	60

10:2 60
10:3   63, 81, 86, 91, 96, 100, 101
10:4 . . . . 100, 105
10:5ff. 14
10:5–8 10
13:33 151
13:55 63
15:15 51
15:24 . . . . 8, 14
16:15–16 51
16:17 . . . . 39, 42
16:18–19 52
17:1 51
17:24–27 51
18:12–14 14
18:21 51
19:21 84
19:27 51
19:28 25
20:20–21 68
20:22 68
20:28 68
21:31 82
22:37–39 74
26:13 150
26:14–16 105
26:14 105
26:21 105
26:24 105
26:25 105
26:37 51
26:46–50 105
26:46 105
26:47 105
26:48 105
26:50 106
26:75 40
27:3–4 106
27:5 106

27:56 151
27:61 151
28:19ff. 25, 33
28:19 15
28:20 28

Mark

1:16–20 12
1:16–17 54
1:17 . . . . 7, 12–13
1:18 59
1:19 67
1:29ff. 40
1:29 . . . . 51, 67
2:1–12 82
2:13–17 81
2:13–14 82
2:17 83
3:13–18 54
3:13–16 9
3:14–15 150
3:14 . . . . 14, 87
3:17 . . . . 50, 60
3:18 . . . 60, 63, 81, 86, 91, 96,
                       100, 101
3:19 105
5:37 . . . . 51, 67
6:3 63
6:7–13 10
7:24–30 151
8:27 42
8:29 42
8:32–33 42
8:33 . . . . 43, 107
8:34–35 43
8:36–37 43
9:2 . . . . 51, 67
10:32 91
12:29–31 74

13:1-4 56
13:3 67
14:9 150
14:10 105
14:18 105
14:20 105
14:33 . . . . 51, 67
14:66-72 46
15:40 . . . . 63, 151
16:7 52
16:15 15

Luke

1:42 151
1:45 151
2:4 97
2:36-38 151
3:1 86
4:38ff. 40
5 63
5:1-11 . . . . 13, 40
5:1-3 41
5:3 51
5:4-5 41
5:8 41
5:10 . . . . 40, 41
5:27-30 81
5:27 40
6:12-16 9
6:13-16 54
6:13 . . . . 10, 25
6:14 . . . . 60, 86, 96
6:15 . . . . . . 81, 91, 100
6:16 . . . . 101, 105
7:36-50 151
8:2-3 151
8:51 51
9:1-6 . . . . 10, 40
9:28 51

10:23 94
10:27 74
15:1 82
15:4-7 14
15:8-10 151
18:1-8 151
18:11 82
18:13-14 83
19:2 82
22:3 . . . . 105, 106
22:8 67
22:30-31 51
23:31ff. 53
24:34 52
24:47 15
24:48ff. 26

John

1:13 . . . . 60, 63, 101
1:18 89
1:35-42 40
1:36 . . . . 13, 55
1:37-39 55
1:38-39 . . . . 13, 87
1:40-43 55
1:42 . . . . 39, 50
1:44 . . . . 39, 86
1:45 . . . . 86, 97
1:46 . . . . 86, 97
1:47 98
1:48 98
1:49 98
2:1-11 96
2:5 151
3:16 73
4:1-39 151
4:24 72
4:42 98
6:5 88

6:7 88
6:8–9 56
6:12–13 45
6:51 45
6:60 45
6:66–69 46
6:67–69 51
6:70 105
6:71 . . . . 104, 105
7:42 97
8:32 23
10:11ff. 14
11:16 91
12:4 104
12:20–22 88
12:23–24 57
12:6 105
13:1 . . . . 70, 73
13:2 106
13:6 51
13:21 105
13:23 69
13:29 105
13:34 . . . . 17, 74
14:4 92
14:5 92
14:6 92
14:7 89
14:8 89
14:9–11 89
14:9 121
14:22–23 102
15:12 17
15:13 69
15:15 69
16:12–13 45
17:21–22 17
18:2 105
18:5 105

18:10ff. 40
19:25–27 151
19:25 . . . . 63, 69
20:1 152
20:2 69
20:3–10 52
20:4–6 52
20:11–18 152
20:23 10
20:24 91
20:25 93
20:27 93
20:28 93
20:29 93
21:1–13 68
21:2ff. 94
21:2 . . . . 91, 96
21:7 69
21:15 47
21:19 48

Acts

1:8 . . . . 15, 26
1:13–14 54
1:13 63, 81, 86, 91, 96, 100, 101
1:15–26 . . . . 34, 52
1:17 105
1:21–22 108
1:23 107
1:26 107
2:14–40 52
2:42 22
3:1–4 68
3:11 68
3:12–26 52
4:8–12 52
4:13 68
4:19 68
4:20 69

4:36 140
4:37 140
5:1–11 52
5:29 52
5:32 26
6:2–4 135
6:5–6 135
6:8 135
6:11–14 136
7:54 137
7:56 136
7:58 . . . . 110, 137
7:59–60 136
8:1 . . . . 110, 137
8:4 137
8:14–17 52
8:14–15 68
9:4 125
9:14 110
9:15 109
9:17 110
9:27 140
9:31 26
10 52
11:1–18 52
11:19–20 137
11:20 111
11:26 . . . . 111, 137
12:1–2 61
12:17 64
13–14 140
13:1 140
13:3ff. 26
13:3 135
13:13 141
13:21 110
14:23 26
15 53
15:1–35 141

15:13–21 64
15:13 63
15:14 39
15:22 142
15:23 142
15:26 109
15:28 26
15:32 142
15:36–40 141
15:39 141
15:40 142
16:1 129
16:2 130
16:3 130
16:16–40 130
18:2 145
18:3 . . . . 110, 145
18:18 153
18:24–25 143
18:26 143
18:27–28 143
18:27 143
19:22 130
19:23 148
19:29 139
20:4 . . . . 131, 139
20:28 26
20:34 110
21:9 152
21:18 64
22:3 110
22:7 110
22:13 110
26:14 110
27:2 139

Romans

1:1 110
3:24 115

3:28 . . . . 66, 114

5:5 . . . . 20, 122

6:3 116

6:4 116

6:5 116

6:11 116

8:1 116

8:2 . . . . 116, 120

8:9 . . . . 120, 121

8:10 116

8:14 21

8:15 120

8:26–27 121

8:31 117

8:32 107

8:39 . . . . 116, 117

12:5 116

12:11 123

12:17 123

15:24 112

15:28 112

16:1–2 153

16:1 139

16:3–5 148

16:3 . . . . 116, 139, 153

16:6 153

16:7 116

16:9 139

16:10 116

16:12–13 139

16:12 . . . . 139, 154

16:15 154

16:21 131

16:23 147

1 Corinthians

1:1 110

1:2–3 116

1:2 127

1:12 143

1:13 127

1:31 116

2:11 121

2:12 121

3:4–6 143

3:5 144

3:6–9 144

3:16 120

4:6 143

4:12 110

4:14–15 126

4:17 130

9:1 110

9:22 111

10:16–17 18

10:17 126

11:1 113

11:5 152

11:23 35

11:26 25

12:7 126

12:27–30 152

12:27 126

14:24–25 128

14:26 127

14:34 152

15:3–4 35

15:3 31

15:5 . . . . 52, 53

15:7 63

15:9 124

15:32 148

15:45 121

16:10–11 130

16:12 144

16:19 . . . . 139, 146

16:22 80

2 Corinthians

1:1	111
1:5	117
1:8–9	148
1:19	130, 142
1:20	29
1:22	123
3:2	125
3:16—4:6	29
4:6	110
4:10	117
5:5	123
5:14–15	112
7:3	92
7:6–7	132
7:13	132
8:6	132
8:23	132
11:23–28	112
11:28	125
12:13	110
13:5	116
13:14	16, 122

Galatians

1:1	34
1:6	125
1:13	124
1:15–16	110
1:18	34, 53
1:19	63
2:1–10	53
2:3	131
2:7ff.	53
2:9	35, 63, 68
2:11–14	52
2:16	66, 115
2:20	107, 115, 116
3:28	126, 152

Ephesians

4:6	120, 121
4:19	126
5:22	122
6:14	116
1:1	111
1:13–14	123
2:19–22	27
2:20	12
4:3–4	127
4:12	126
4:20	87
5:2	107
5:21–33	127
5:25–33	149
5:25	107
5:30	126
6:21	139

Philippians

1:1	130
1:19	121
2:1	17
2:20	129
2:25	139
3:3	121
3:6	124
3:7–10	111
3:12	110
4:1	125
4:2	154
4:13	117
4:18	139

Colossians

1:1	111
1:7	139
1:24	126

4:7 139	
4:10 139	
4:12 139	
4:15 147	

1 Thessalonians

2:7–8 126
3:1–2 130
5:19 127

1 Timothy

4:14 . . . . 26, 135
5:22 135

2 Timothy

1:5 130
1:6 135
1:12 118
1:14 31
3:15 130
4:10 132
4:12 139
4:19 139

Titus

1:4 131
1:5 132
3:8 133
3:12 . . . . 132, 139

Philemon

1 130
2 . . . . 147, 153
23 139

Hebrews

11:1 94
13:23 131

James

1:1 64
1:27 66
2:26 66
4:15 66

1 Peter

1:8–9 49
2:25 35
5:1 48
5:12 143

2 Peter

1:1 39

1 John

1:1ff. 21
1:1–3 14
1:2 18
1:3 18
1:5 72
1:6ff. 19
1:7 73
2:1–2 73
2:19 21
3:20 107
4:8 72
4:16 72

2 John

9–11 21

Jude

1 102
8 102
11 102
12–13 102
20–22 103
24–25 103

Revelation

1:1 76
1:4 76
1:9 76
1:10 77
5:4 78
5:6 77
19:6–7 80
21:14 12
22:8 76
22:20 80